HISTORY LOST HISTORY
FOUND SERIES

BOOK ONE

MY GRANDMOTHER RODE A HORSE

Robin A. Roberts Harris, M.Ed.

MY GRANDMOTHER RODE A HORSE

Library of Congress Control Number: 2019918528

FIRST EDITION

Cover design by Robin A. Roberts Harris

DEDICATION

This book is dedicated to all the women whom reside within my genes, my mother and her foremothers and my father and his foremothers.

Photograph from artwork in my private collection.

TABLE OF CONTENTS

FOR MY MOTHER

Kay Hankerson holding her daughter, Robin 1958

PART ONE

INTRODUCTION - The Search Begins

When I decided to start researching my genealogical tree it was because I wanted to know the people in my family as well as their stories. I was curious about how they ended up in their various locations, their occupations and of course, their place within the family. I wanted to know the stories of my ancestors, their customs and traditions, and I especially wanted to see how far back I could get in order to, I guess, find myself. I believe this might be a part of maturity, taking a closer look at who you are and how you got that way. I wanted to learn my history, or I should say 'herstory'. To find the people inside me. What about the women? They have names but finding them within their families is difficult. As I continued to build the family tree, it seemed to me that the women were ignored, their stories were hidden behind the patrilineal family tree and secondary, only important because of the children they produced. I also wondered, how do you write about the pain of physical abuse, sexual abuse, or infidelity within a marriage, multiple marriages, an outside child, [southern term than means an illegitimate child, one born to someone other than your wife, outside the marriage] and divorce? I wanted to know the women's stories. I wanted to find out how they fit into the family legacy, after all there would be no history without them.

Have you ever wondered what influence your ancestors have in your life just by the virtue of the genes you share? I recently looked at a picture of my great grandmother, she looked so familiar to me despite the fact she died before I was born. What else did Elsie leave with me? There is no part of you that is not an accumulation of the past, of all the people, in all the parts of your family ... your health, your physical appearance, your mental or psychic ability, and your very being.

I am the oldest daughter of an oldest daughter, and the oldest granddaughter. I must admit I am very much like my mother. We are very quick thinkers, we speak our minds, and we both are very family oriented and stubborn. I had one sister, Sharon, and we were raised together. That might seem a silly thing to say but these days families are often blended or separated.

It is very fortunate being the first. I have a baby book that contains many pictures of me with my parents, grandparents and other family members; these photographs chronicle my life as I grew within my family. This is not to say my sister did not have these things just not to the same degree. What happens is the first child creates a wonder of life, something beautiful, unexpected, familiar yet unfamiliar. This baby creates a new part of the family and at the same time creates a family unit of your own. Subsequent children lose that 'first child' exhilaration. My mother made up a small family tree based on the information she was given. This was very useful when I began my research

I began to wonder more about my family while in high school when I had a project. I remember asking my mother, enough questions that I could see an outline of the family up to my great grandparents on my mom's paternal side. As I got older, I had conversations with my mother who knew her father's family very well.

In my own life, work and raising my family sidelined my research efforts. Until 1995 when I was diagnosed with an auto immune disease, Systemic Lupus Erythematosus (SLE). My symptoms were in the form of an inflammatory arthritis and extreme fatigue. After being diagnosed and beginning treatment I suddenly had a flare, or activation of the disease. One month after my diagnosis, I saw my rheumatologist on a Wednesday and was scheduled for an appointment on Friday with the nephrologist. I went into my appointment Friday, unbeknownst to me, in kidney failure, stage 3 [in two days!] and began treatment. Without this appointment I would not have survived the weekend. I retired that year from the Detroit Police Department and concentrated on staying alive! Following a year and a half of chemotherapy treatments I moved to the hot, dry, sunny state of Arizona. My physician believed the dry climate would be a benefit to the painful symptoms I was experiencing and speaking honestly, I needed a change in my life.

Soon after my move to Arizona one tragedy struck after another. I felt like my family was falling apart. I filed for divorce from a short lived marriage, this was followed by the untimely death of my sister's daughter, the loss of my Grandmother's sisters, [two Big aunts, which some people refer to as great aunts] Aunt Elaine, who was the closest thing I had to a grandmother on my father's side of the family, her sister, Aunt Violet, and then my sister's shocking murder. In my sister's case, the family was not aware of the circumstances of her being physically abused by her husband. After she filed for divorce she was stalked by her husband. Although she filed a restraining order; he did not stop until he found her and killed her. I tried to hold my family together while also working through my own grief and pain. I did not again look at any genealogical documents until after I graduated with my

Bachelor of Arts degree in Women's Studies [with minors in Psychology and Sociology] and got married the next day in 2000. I obtained a Master of Education degree in Counseling two years later to the day.

In 1998, not quite a year after the death of my sister, I decided to take my mom and niece, Marissa on a road trip to Cambridge, Guernsey County, Ohio, the place my grandmother might have been born but was raised. It was a genealogy field trip, something to take our minds away from the previous year. Recently I found inspiration that I thought my mother would appreciate:

> *I wanted to tell her that her life will not go back, that she will never be the same, because a piece of her left with her child. And that even though the pain does not go away, somehow her soul will eventually make enough room so she can hold it all– the grief, the pain, the joy and the love.*
>
> *Costello*

I now lived in Arizona, 2,000 miles away from Michigan, where I was born and raised. Arizona has mountains, which seem to change with the weather; majestic most days. When they are covered with clouds, mostly in the winter, it makes them look magical. During the monsoon season in the evenings they can appear dark and ominous. In Arizona the days are bright, sunny, with blue skies and the climate is hot, often very hot and dry. Instead of the lush green of fields and trees, cloudy skies and humidity I now have desert and cacti. I have never had the need for a winter coat since I moved to this climate. This visit to Ohio, where my grandmother was raised, had the benefit of reminding me of memories of the climate where I grew up and let me embrace the breathtaking scenery. It reminded me how I much I love the country, woods, water, the sound of the birds, and the feel of the wind. We did not realize that the juncture from U.S. 70 to U.S. 40 put us on the National Road also known as the National Pike.

The National Road, also known as Route 40 and the National Pike, was completed across Guernsey County in 1828. It was the first Federally funded road in United States history. It was designated as a historic road in 2002. Later in this story you will learn the importance and impact that this road had for my family. It was interesting to see the county's homes and buildings while passing through the small towns, we thought about stopping at one of the small diners but decided maybe on the way back. My niece saw some children walking through Cambridge and they were not wearing shoes; my mother explained that was something you see in a small town and rarely, if ever in cities.

That day was quite a learning experience. From the Guernsey county courthouse, I was able to find my grandmother's original 'card'; it looked like an index card and contained the information of her birth; this information was later transcribed into a legal birth record index. I also found and copied wills, transfers of land and many other documents. I obtained copies of everything I could find that contained family names that I knew at that time. Mom visited the Guernsey County genealogical society and copied pages from books, gathered information and documents, as well as met and talked to the staff. Apparently, one of the women had looked for old grave markers and located some at a location nearby. These places they explored held not headstones, but stones, marking burial for what would have been from 'our people'. She pointed us towards a house not far away. Her instructions led us to a location where behind the rear of the property, after the clearing, at the end of the woods, all the way in the back were the markers, where we would have to put our hands in the dirt to find them. We did go to look to see what the area looked like. The location was just as had been described. We would have had to go all the way to the back, about a quarter of a mile, through a field and behind a woodsy area to find the burial spots and my mother was, and is, afraid of snakes and would not venture farther.

Soon after I moved to Arizona, I began the lost tradition of writing letters to family members. My mother told me I should write a book because she enjoyed the descriptions of the environment here and hearing about the culture of the city. One day I decided it was time to once again start working on my family tree. I organized my desk and got to work. I pulled out all my boxes, files, books and papers. I was shocked at the amount of documentation that I had obtained in Ohio in 1998! Because I had been working on a computer during my coursework it was easy to start a family tree with the old and new information I had. Numerous trips were made as I began to visit Family History Centers, close to home, and in Mesa, Arizona. I also attended research seminars, both in person and online as well as jamborees. I conducted research, examining rolls and rolls of film searching for my family on my mother's side. At some point my mother and I booked a trip for Salt Lake City, Utah where we found answers to the questions, we were looking for. She was researching her father's side of the family while I examined her mother's side. We had a wonderful trip as the hotel and a restaurant were right next door to the Family

History Library. We did not sleep much; it could wait until we got home.

My mother wanted to 'get back to Africa' with the family lineage so she took a test sometime later to determine her female ancestry. She was quite surprised; I would even say aghast when she received the results. It determined we, the women of this family, were not at all what we thought.

"The mitochondrial DNA (mtDNA) sequence that we determined from your sample is of European Ancestry. Your sequence belongs to a non-African lineage. We understand that this information may be difficult to absorb, especially if you were not aware of a European ancestry on your mother's maternal lineage, it does not mean you are not African American."

Explaining DNA

Deoxyribonucleic acid (DNA) is a molecule that contains the biological instructions that make each species unique. This molecule is composed of two chains that coil around each other to form a double helix carrying genetic instruction for development, functioning, and growth which is passed from adult organisms to their offspring during reproduction.

DNA is found inside a special area of the cell called the nucleus; therefore, it is often referred to as nuclear DNA. Because the cell is very small, and because organisms have many DNA molecules per cell, each DNA molecule must be tightly packaged. This packaged form of the DNA is called a chromosome.

The complete DNA instruction book, or genome, for a human contains about 3 billion bases and about 20,000 genes on 23 pairs of chromosomes.

Besides the DNA located in the nucleus, humans have a small amount of DNA in cell structures known as mitochondria. Mitochondria generate the energy the cell needs to function properly. In sexual reproduction, humans inherit approximately half of their nuclear DNA from the male parent and approximately half from the female parent. However, we inherit ALL the mitochondrial DNA from the female parent. This occurs because only egg cells, and not sperm cells, keep their mitochondria during fertilization. Females typically have two of the same classification of sex chromosome, XX and males typically have two different classifications of sex chromosomes XY.

When we take a DNA test to determine our ancestry it can be one of several types: mtDNA, [mitochondrial], Y-DNA [paternal] or Autosomal testing.

Mitochondrial DNA is passed down from your biological mother's egg, your biological father shares none of his mitochondria with you. This is the reason why you can only trace your biological mother's female line using mtDNA testing.

Y-DNA tests look at one of the chromosomes in the 23rd pair, the Y chromosome. The Y chromosome is passed directly from a person's biological father, who inherited it from his biological father, and so on. Women do not have a Y chromosome. This makes the Y chromosome useful for tracing the male line as well as for evidence that another male may be related.

Autosomal DNA tests measure 22 pairs of chromosomes called the autosomes. Autosomal DNA testing analyzes the largest part of your DNA that comes from your parents. The information in these chromosomes can help identify recent and distant relatives and find the places your ancestors lived 500 to 1000 or more years ago. Autosomal DNA testing can reveal more about your ethnicity and who you are related to.

Let's Talk About Definitions

I had known there was White ancestry on my grandmother's side of the family but to be honest it never occurred to me that it was important enough to consider. My Aunt Elsie looked White to me, in my family it was described as, 'quite fair', my grandmother was brown, her brother, Uncle Pete [Lawrence] was a bit lighter color than she with an olive quality or tone to his skin. Quite frankly when I was young, I thought babies just came out and you got what you got, regarding color. I didn't really think much about race until we moved to Detroit where I started high school. I rather quickly had to evaluate my 'Blackness'. I realized my hair was on the thin side like my mothers. I would have to wash it, braid it, and curl it in order to have an afro. It also did not help that I spoke "proper English". I was called 'redbone' [in other words, not quite done]. I was asked 'are you Black or White' and where are you from? I did not like the city; for me it was a culture shock.

The United States Federal Census, for some time periods defined people as Black, White, Mulatto and Indian; I have attached a chart of their classifications.

1790		1800		1820	
Free white males		1800 Free white males		1820 Free white males, free white females	
Free white females		1810 Free white females		1830 Free colored males and females	
Slaves		All other free persons		1840 Slaves	
		Slaves			

1850	1860	1870 / 1880	1920
White	White or Black	1870 White	White
Black	Mulatto	1880 Black	Black
Mulatto	Black slaves	Mulatto	Mulatto
Black slaves	Mulatto slaves	Indian	Other
Mulatto slaves	Indian	Chinese	Indian
			Chinese
			Japanese
			Filipino
			Korean
			Hindu

1890	1900	1910	1930 / 1940
White	White	White	1930 White
Black	Black (Negro or of Negro descent)	Black	1940 Negro
Mulatto	Indian	Mulatto	Other
Quadroon	Chinese	Other	Indian
Octoroon	Japanese	Indian	Chinese
Indian		Chinese	Japanese
Chinese		Japanese	Filipino
Japanese			Korean
			Hindi

Mulatto: Definitions varied from census to census, but this term generally means someone who is black and at least one other race.
Quadroon: Someone with "one-fourth black blood," according to census-taker instructions.
Octoroon: Someone with "one-eighth or any trace of black blood," according to census-taker instructions.
In 1910, the vast majority of the Other category were Korean, Filipino and Asian Indian (called Hindu)
1960 onward: People could choose their own race.
2000 onward: Americans could be recorded in more than one race category on the census form.

In the 1870 Census, my great-great grandmother's entire family was listed as White. I believe it is the result of the census taker looking at the mother, Susan. Obviously, the census taker did not know the family because on the far right side of the page someone had noted "the family cannot attend school on account of color" Further down on the same page were my great-great uncle and his family also listed in White with the same notation.

As I research further back into the family, I must look at all the records, rather than sort them as Black or White, it makes it difficult and time consuming. I cannot research within the parameters of race because I never know what color they might be defined as at any time; I do not know what the perceptions of the writers of documents saw when they looked at my people.

What I find amusing is the White relatives, my distant family members, whom I have found, through research, were told the same story of having 'Indian' blood, Cherokee, to be exact. These folks were also surprised to find out, during research when they came upon the term, Mulatto; and later they discovered that their families were slaves. It made life very interesting for them when the primary researcher notified the family of the stories their blood told.

I was always told that my grandmother's sisters were 'very fair' and when my mother showed me a picture of her aunt's first born daughter, Elsie Green, her favorite cousin in Pittsburg, it was clear she also had a very light, fair complexion and soft fine hair like my grandmother. My mother, and I also inherited our hair texture and thin lips from the female ancestors before us.

My mother's favorite cousin Elsie Greene 1910-1986

The search for the generations of my female forbears
continues. I have learned to read the women between the
lines. I developed the idea for History Lost/History Found
book series because of how distinct each of the branches of
my family tree are; some are very large and full, while others
are totally broken. An example are the lost stories of my great
grandfather, Lawrence Busby and his birth family. It seems
to me he lived his life in italics with no true heritage to tell of
his past because of his peculiar circumstance. The search for
all these branches continues within my, and other family

members, DNA. I intend to find the histories. The research goes on.

PREFACE

I SEE DEAD PEOPLE AND THEY ARE MY ANCESTORS

When I was young, I started having dreams that were so real I thought I was awake, until I did wake up. Many times, these dreams were prophetic. If I dreamed of something that could cause me harm, I generally was aware of it when it started to happen the way I dreamt it. Talk about déjà vu! It was something that really was scary for me for a while, but I eventually saw the blessing in it. As I grew older, I would just know things. There were many times that my son's school had the phone in their hand to call me just as I phoned them. Often, I have called someone or texted them just as they were picking up the phone to call or text me. My oldest son always tells his wife "you might as well call her before she calls us, she knows when something is wrong"; and I do usually call before they get around to it. My youngest son jokes that I have antennae.

When I worked for the police department, I found part of this ability of seeing could be quite devastating. This is the most heart wrenching example. I dreamt I was in a patrol car, in route to assist another police vehicle in a chase; our car was

19

hit, on my side, I saw the car too late, the car was knocked sideways onto a porch, with extreme force, it just happened so fast and all went black. I woke up shaking, in a cold sweat. The next morning the news struck me like a brick "Officer Hubbard was killed when her patrol car was struck at 2:20 a.m. in front of 2402 Canton Street by a vehicle being chased following a robbery attempt. Officer Hubbard was assisting the units when the patrol car was broadsided by the vehicle, which was driving at an estimated 90 mph. Officer Hubbard was killed at the scene and her partner was injured." Vikki Hubbard was my friend! I had never been so traumatized; I lived her death in a dream.

What was even more difficult was not knowing if who I was seeing was me. Eventually, I developed a trick, I started to look for and find a mirror in the dream and see if it the face was mine.

This gift, or blessing, seeing in my dreams saved me from being severely injured. I dreamt that, while working on patrol, I was chasing a man on foot and saw myself being violently stabbed by him in the leg; I was bleeding profusely before all went black. The area was a field and I could not find him or see him because he was hiding in the tall weeds. When I experienced this event happening, I did not chase him into the weeds rather I requested a unit with a dog to locate him.

My partner was shocked because I never had done this during this type of situation at any other time.

With my family incidents like this these things happened all the time. My mother told me that she was ill once and had not shared this with the family. According to her, I came to her house one morning and told her, [my deceased grandfather] Papa said, "don't worry everything will be ok". I don't recall this incident but there are a few I do remember. Sometimes for no reason I smell my grandfather's pipe and I know he is there checking on me.

Prior to my sister's daughter's, Alexis' death, I dreamed a child playing in tall grass. There was a man with an instrument, like a scythe cutting the grass down in another area. The child was laughing, jumping and falling all around, having the time of her life. It was a beautiful day with a blue sky, and a soft breeze blowing. I heard a voice calling in the distance and when I looked, I saw a woman sitting on the patio, at a long table snapping beans. The patio was attached to the house in the back. The man started walking towards the porch, I followed, and he sat in one of those old swings, that moved back and forth. I went to him, sat down and laid my head in his lap, and he rubbed my head. I felt a contentment that I never have before and then, I woke up. Shortly afterward my niece, my sister's second daughter died.

Later, when I relayed this story to my mother, she said I described her grandparent's and their house to a tee. I told her it must have been a message that Alexis, my niece [the little child in the dream], was with them and happy. I had never met my great grandparents on my mom's father's side because they both died before I was born. My mother complained, "nobody ever comes to see me, they all come to see you?" My response was that I just wish I knew who the man was who was always at the foot of my bed when I'm sleeping. I told her the first time it happened I heard my grandmother tell me, "it's okay", so I rolled over and went back to sleep. Mom asked me to describe him, and his clothing to her, which I did, then she went to the basement. When she returned, she had a box of pictures; she searched through until she found one and gave it to me. It was the man! I asked her who he was, and she told me it was my grandmother' s brother, Jonah. I said, "he never saw me why he would stand at the end of my bed now and not say anything"? My mom informed me that he saw me as an infant, he didn't say anything just watched me sleeping, at the foot of my crib. She also told me that he was a hermit, had no children and he did not talk very much. I now believe he was watching over me, my angel.

I had a recent experience that was very eerie. I was washing a crystal vase that was my grandmother's, my favorite. Suddenly it slipped and then it seemed as time slowed down. I watched the vase break on my tile countertop slowly, inch by inch. There was glass everywhere. I couldn't figure out how that vase made so much glass. It was in my hair, my clothes, all around me. It took a long time to clean up and I continued to question how it spread to the places in and on me. Later that evening my mother called to tell me my Aunt had been in a car accident. When I spoke to Aunt Joanne [who I refer to as Googie], she told me about the accident and said, "I don't know where all that glass came from, glass was everywhere, my hair, my clothes, my shoes, even my underwear". I do not know how it works but I believe I had that experience of glass *occurred at the exact time* my Aunt had that accident. Although her car was totaled, she was safe. I wonder if my grandmother saved her.

So, if that was not enough for you to question my sanity, I also remember incidents from past lives.

I can remember things and I know they occurred long ago. It is very difficult to explain, like remembering something from when you are a child and you know it is true, but it can baffle you without confirmation or someone else explaining the circumstances. These memories are not enough for me to be

23

specific but enough to know it was me, or, I now believe, one of the people in my DNA.

I clearly remember living in a house with my father and we lived near a stream that ran just before a forest of trees. I do not remember much about him other than he was a strict man and could be mean. I remember that I did not speak English. I played the piano which was in a large room with beautiful wood floors. I could see the woods from my window, which was not on the first floor. It is amazing to me that I can still smell the trees. The woods were thick and made up of cypress trees, tall, dark and majestic. How could I ever forget? There was something about that smell that gave a sense of safety and security as if nothing could harm me so long as the smell permeated the area. I rode horses along the stream taking in the fresh clean scent, free from the troubles of the world. I remember arguing with my father, I refused to marry. He pushed me...I hit my head; it was dark.

Another memory is of being a young woman, a slave. There is something on my neck, maybe a cuff, scars; I do not know. I remember that I had the gift of seeing [the future]. I knew what would happen if I were found out if they knew of this gift. I would be used to their advantage or worse, they would think me a witch or demon and kill me. So, I walked into the ocean and drowned. I have tried to figure out a time period, but I cannot. What I remember more than anything are the walks I took along the shore. I have no memory of anyone, with or around me, and it is bewildering. I can hear the water beating against the shore, smell it and feel the humidity of the air. When I walked into the water it was cold, I could not breathe but did not fight. I had no intention of coming out of the water alive. I have had déjà vu when I walk near southern cities off the ocean on the east coast. I believe I must have been in that area a long time ago. The sound of the Atlantic Ocean is frightening to me but strikes a feeling of awe, nevertheless.

Finally, I have a memory that is like flashes. This is from a very long time ago. I can only describe it like something you might see on television as if you get brief, intermittent clips, or see things so fast you must have known what came before to be able to picture what you are seeing. We are nomadic. I am dancing in bare feet, there are tents, there is a fire, other women, a man who sees over me. There are hands around my throat, I am being choked, and finally blackness.

IS THIS REAL?

I have questioned myself about the reality of the above circumstances and wonder if they are in fact memories. While I cannot say for sure that I believe in reincarnation, I do know that I do not want to come back here anymore. The idea of inherited, or genetic memory seems to have some degree of plausibility. Episodic memory is of specific events, as in things that are important to you. I remember a doll as tall as me that my mother gave me, and I remember trying to get her downstairs with me to the basement; however, I don't remember the circumstances around receiving her, was it my birthday, Christmas, I do not know. Semantic memory is of information, facts, such as, you know who the President is and who was President before him. Lastly, Procedural memory is remembering how to do things like riding a bike or brushing your teeth. Procedural memory can be inherited, and it is clearly genetic. An example is how babies know how to suck without being taught to do it.

I question if it possible for all three types of these memories be inherited. Carl Gustav Jung, 1875-1961, a Swiss psychotherapist and psychiatrist, and the founder of analytical psychology is known for his theory of the *collective unconscious*. The collective unconscious defines his broader concept of inherited traits, intuitions and collective wisdom of the past. It is a type of genetic memory that can be shared by individuals with a common ancestor or history. According to Jung, the collective unconscious consists of implicit beliefs and thoughts had by our ancestors. We would not be aware of this belief, but it would influence how we behave. As an example, if our ancestors had a belief that dogs were dangerous, this collective unconscious passed to us would influence how we conduct ourselves in a specified way when we are near or see a dog. Another example, if our ancestors wore chains on their wrists or necks, we might have an abhorrence for adornments in those areas.

Jung came upon his theory of the collective unconscious during psychoanalysis of his patients' dreams. He believed that the symbolism that was prominent in their dreams often bore marks of a specific ancestral history which was difficult to explain by anything in the dreamer's own life.

If in fact, there is such a thing as genetic memory how is it passed on? This is a question I asked my friend, Anna because she is a scientist. I like to ask her questions because she never looks at me like I am crazy when I explain these strange experiences to her. She was not much help with answers, but she did point out that all my past lives were as women. I had never really considered that point although I do believe it is important. The most important set of genetic instructions we all get comes from our DNA, passed down through the generations.

Since we discussed DNA earlier, and more specifically the MtDNA, I wonder if this could be the means, or is that specific chromosome the means by which memories from the women before me are passed to me?

Scientists have observed epigenetic memories passed down for fourteen generations. These kinds of genetic changes were observed in roundworms. I know, I know. Epigenetics is the study of inherited changes in gene expression. In recent years scientists have learned that we do not only inherit our parents' genetic information we also inherit other information through cells' epigenetic memory. Traumatic events, such as the Dutch famine, the Holocaust, and Slavery may cause effects on subsequent generations. The current study conducted on worms may lead to the how the epigenetic responses, that are inherited, follow an active process that gets passed on through generations and hopefully will lead to a more comprehensive theory on gene heredity as well as memory in humans.

PART ONE

MY MOTHER AND HER MOTHERS

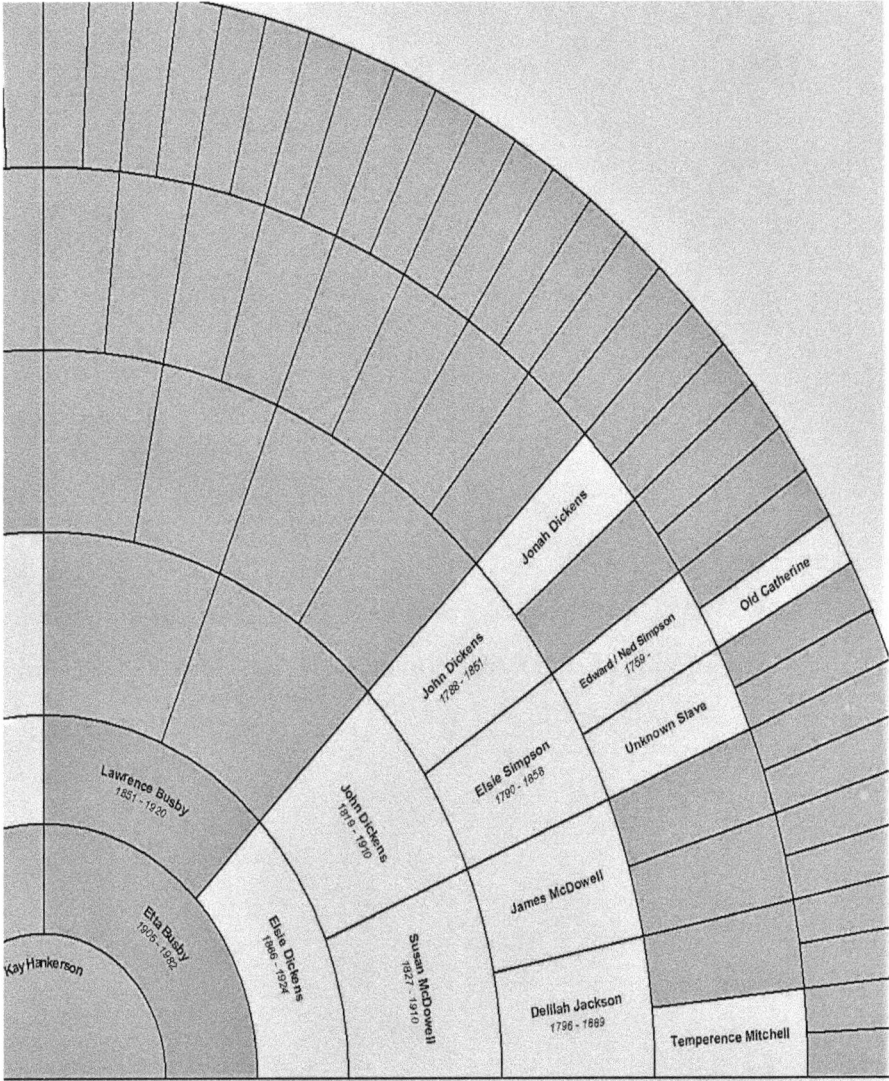

Kay Hankerson

Etta Busby
1905 - 1982

Lawrence Busby
1851 - 1920

Elsie Dickens
1886 - 1924

John Dickens
1819 - 1910

John Dickens
1786 - 1851

Jonah Dickens

Elsie Simpson
1790 - 1856

Edward / Ned Simpson
1759 -

Old Catherine

Unknown Slave

Susan McDowell
1827 - 1910

James McDowell

Delilah Jackson
1796 - 1889

Temperence Mitchell

My mother, Kay Hankerson and me, her daughter, Robin, 1958

MY MOTHER

Kay Hankerson (Living)

What do you write about your mother? I asked Mom what to write about her and she said, "whatever you want". While her response was not helpful, I did get a chuckle. My mother is a strong woman, very independent and part gypsy. If she is not comfortable where she is, she will move. Whether in the city, or out of the state she will leave if she feels the need. Typically, the mother daughter-relationship is not like any other in many ways. It is often because the two of them share a great deal of characteristics. The mother has shaped her daughter in her image, and a mother does not ever believe her child is going to grow up. That creates a push/pull of control and independence that generally starts when the daughter enters puberty. Being the oldest daughter, as best I could, I often held things back from my mom that I knew would cause her concern and/or pain. In that respect, we have very much in common.

My mother was very close to both of her parents. She has told me several stories about growing up in the household and her relationships with her grandparents and her sisters, Googie [my nickname for Joanne] and Sharon, my sister's namesake. As the oldest my mom was fearless. She enjoyed her young life and her family doted on her.

Listed on the 1940 in Inkster, Wayne County, Michigan Census are my grandparents, my mother and boarders, a married couple and an additional border are listed. My grandmother had a two-story brick house with, at one time, a white picket fence. It had large back yard with a garden, apple tree, rhubarb, grape vines and at one time there were chickens. There was also a barbeque pit that my grandfather built. Mom told me a story about how she would tell her babysitter, "that's not where that belongs, that's not how my mama does it", etc. She was a bossy little one, even at a young age she always spoke her mind. Her childhood seems to me typical of a two-parent household. Her mother was Catholic, and her paternal grandfather was a Baptist minister, so she attended both churches before going to her grandparent's house where they spent every Sunday after church. Her parents were loving but firm. She had a fat, yellow cat named Chicken. Mom relates that when they needed new shoes, she would put on her most beat up pair and go to her father's barbershop. She would tell him she and her sisters needed shoes, and of course, he would send her back to her mother with money to buy them. My mother had tuberculosis at some point when she was younger and was hospitalized for it.

My mother apparently also had a smart mouth, she says, she was 'flip' when she was older, probably during those dreaded teens. When her mother called, she answered, "what" instead of 'yes ma'am' which got her in a great deal of trouble. She had to learn respect as each of us should. My mother and her sisters all had chores that were rotated between them. The kitchen included dishes, wiping everything and sweeping the floor; in the living and dining room it was dusting, including the blinds; upstairs was cleaning the bathroom and making your own bed, and being responsible for keeping the room clean. Mom tells a story about how she wanted to go out to a football game one afternoon and her chore was the kitchen and the dishes needed to do be washed. She didn't want to do them because she would be late, so she hid them in the drawers and the oven. Unfortunately for her my grandmother knew what she did. Her mother pulled every dish out of every cabinet, and every piece of silverware out of the drawers and she had to wash them and missed her extracurricular activity. She had permission to drive when she was fifteen. Her instructions by her parents was "do not to leave the town where they lived"; of course, she did to go roller skating, and got caught and grounded. There are many stories that mom has relayed about herself to me.

The only struggle that I know for sure my mother had growing up was her father's infidelity, which embarrassed her. He had an outside daughter that my mother formed a relationship with later in life. Despite this she had a very close relationship with her father. She knew she could always depend on both of her parents. She attended high school in Detroit and if the weather was bad, she would spend the night at her grandparents' home. She is so very thankful her parents and grandparents were strict and taught her how to hold her tongue, or she would have not been the woman she grew into or had a profession as a Stenographer. Mom moved through the ranks in the court, working with the Chief Judge and retiring as a Court Administrator.

My aunts have always been very important in my life. They taught me how to dance, tie my shoes, and develop a love of reading. They were always there for me emotionally. Aunt Googie was a registered nurse who worked as a Surgical Cardiac Nurse. She obtained a degree in Clinical Psychology and worked as a Therapist. Later, she moved out of state and worked as an Educator. She has one daughter, Kay, named after my mother, and she also has a daughter, Amanda.

My Aunt Sharon had a bad heart; and although she was pampered in her younger years, she had a full life, and worked as a Logistic Analyst for General Motors in Detroit. She loved people, being social and liked loud restaurants. She died from Pancreatic Cancer. She had a son, named after her father, Joseph as well as a set of twins, Charles and Jessica. Her daughter has a daughter, Nieema, and one granddaughter, Max.

My parents met at a party. After a courting period they fell in love and married. I recently had a conversation with a member of the clergy recently and we spoke of the first-born child. He explained that first children, for some strange reason, do not always come at the traditional time; it seems they are independent in all ways. Only the subsequent children take nine months to be born. My parents got along well, but sadly divorced when I was young and soon after my sister was born. My father quit his job and as a result of not working he was no longer acting as a provider. Of course, in many relationships there are always reasons that are not spoken of. Daddy's aunt, Jean lived with them and I suspect two queens cannot live in the same castle and that contributed to the divorce. In conversations with my father when he was older, he expressed regret at not having the communication skills to express his feelings and explain his reasoning for his decision to stop working. He always told me he never stopped loving my mother.

My mother worked, went to school and did the best she could to raise her daughters as a single parent. She had many struggles and, at some point, decided to move home, to her parent's house so we, her children, would be around family. She worked and attended business school to become a stenographer. Mom graduated and her picture, noting her graduation and certification from the school, was posted in the Legal News. We all moved back to Detroit and she had a very fulfilling career. Even after moving from home, my mother spoke to her mother every day and her father regularly until they passed.

Kay Hankerson 2008

MY GRANDMOTHER RODE A HORSE

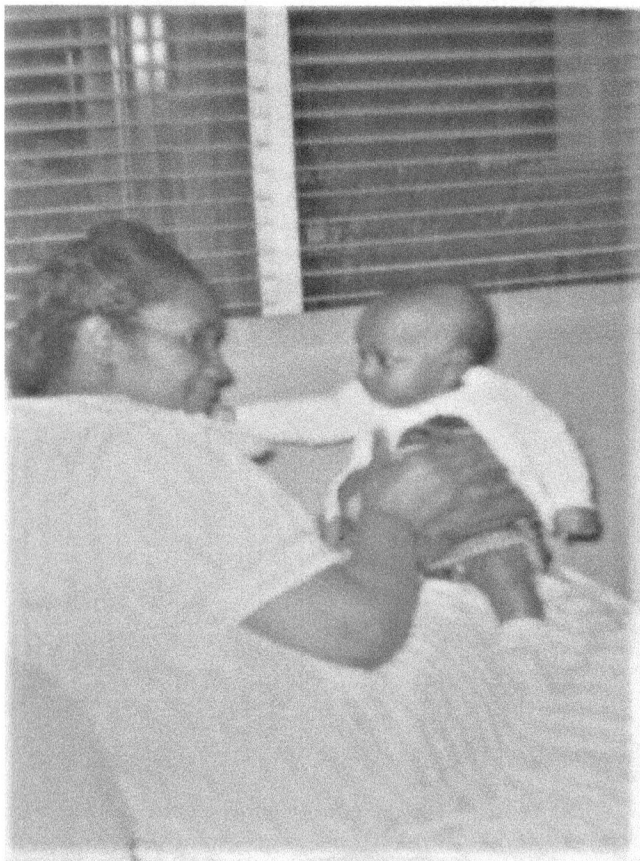

Etta Busby Hankerson and her first grandchild, Robin 1958

My Grandmother

Etta Busby (1905-1982)

My grandmother had soft brown skin, long black hair, cascading down her back that she could sit on, and kind eyes. She was the youngest in her family while I was the oldest child of her first child. She was Catholic and I also was confirmed in the Catholic faith. When I asked Nanny, my name for her, about life when she was growing up, she told me that she rode a horse to go to town. That is what I remember, more than anything, of the stories she told me about her childhood. This was so significant that when I saw the picture used in the beginning of the book, I had to have it. I was trying to remember other stories but very little came to mind. For the most part, what I remember came from other family members. My mother told me the story of how my grandmother would read the newspaper to her father in the morning and he would later discuss it with the guys when he went to work, "word for word" she said, "he had a photostatic memory and so did my mother"[also known as Eidetic Memory the ability to remember an image in so much detail, clarity, and accuracy that it is as though the image were still being perceived]. My mother told me a story about how she was studying one day and needed to go back and look something up. She said my grandmother told her what book, and what page; she only needed to see something once and it was never forgotten. My grandmother did not want any discussion about her age; according to my mother it was because, "she told so many 'stories' [about her age]. She loved to dance, worked as a hairdresser at one time and played the organ and piano. I do remember seeing her dressed in white, in her nurse's uniform.

My grandparents were always in my life and I was not aware of any friction in their relationship. I had a close relationship with both; however, it is obvious that there was some type of discord because after 38 years of marriage Nanny divorced her husband.

It is a common custom to name the firstborn girl after her great grandmother. However, it is clear my grandmother did not want me to have her mother's name because she told my mother "it was something like "Ail-sa [sic]." While researching I found that clearly, she knew her mother's name when she got married and I am quite sure she did not forget it. I wonder why she did not want me to have her mother's name and if it had to do with the number of women in the family with that name or something else.

Immediate memories of Nanny include my watching her cook and the things she taught me, like learning how to crochet, knit, and play gin rummy while we laughed and drank tea at the kitchen table. I remember helping her make wine; which she said she learned from her father, and my sister sipping and getting incredibly drunk, until she was sick. Memories flood back when I scratch the dandruff from my scalp and I recall sitting between her legs to have this done or when I need to straighten my hair for a particular hair style and I see that hot comb, feel it on the back of my neck, 'the kitchen', as she called it. I remember her French braiding my hair. Now I know how much her arthritic hands must have hurt, because she passed 'Arthur-itis' on to me. I clearly remember teasing her about her being short because I got my father's height and towered over her. On my wall I have a piece of art, a young, Black girl, wearing a hat, going to market on a horse; it so reminded me of my grandmother that I used it in the front of this book. Many days I try to imagine what it was like. It is amazing how one story, one memory can send you on a study of genealogy that lasts decades.

Aunt Elsie was my grandmother's niece, the oldest daughter of Nanny's sister, Nancy. She was of course, named after her grandmother. Aunt Elsie and Nanny grew up together, like sisters, in her mother's house. I thought she lived with my grandmother until I recently after a conversation with my mother. However, Aunt Elsie visited with my grandmother frequently for as long as I can remember and until Nanny died, they were close. Later in talking to my mother I found that there was strife between my Nanny and Aunt Elsie. Again, I must say there just cannot be two queens in one castle; apparently, Aunt Elsie moved out when my mother and her sisters were young, although they remained close the rest of their lives (as sister's do).

I have one picture of Aunt Elsie. I have clear memories of us going on walks. Strolling across the streets, up the hill, over the railroad tracks and on to the main avenue are very clear. Looking at the area now it is much further than I imagined. Sometimes it was a little warm and humid and as a result we would work up a little sweat, and other times we would have to bundle up, although I don't ever remember being out in the winter. I loved being outside. The trees, greenery and cloudy days with a breeze were my favorite things while walking along the many paved and unpaved paths. My love of walking, especially now, invokes these memories. Walking is what I do for relaxation, as well as exercise at this time of my life, and it is a result of my travels around town with her. Oftentimes, she would sneak me a piece of candy and I would keep it our secret. The walking is my most impactful memory of her, other than her weight. She was fat, unlike everyone else in the family.

Elsie Jackson Dennard 1909-1984, 1973

In the 1930 U.S. Federal Census, (hereby known as the Census) Nanny and Elsie are listed together as roomers in Detroit, Michigan. Their occupations are both listed as maids for a private family. I was aware that my grandmother had worked for the Henry Ford family as a Nanny for their children. My great grandmother, Elsie had also cared for the Ford children during summers, before her death. This census entry indicates to me that she and Aunt Elsie probably started employment with this family as maids.

Etta Busby Hankerson c. 1960

NOT MY NAMESAKE

Elsie Dickens Busby c. 1885

Elsie Dickens Busby c.1915

My Great Grandmother

Elsie Dickens (1866-1924)

My great-grandmother had six children, two were old enough to be my grandmother's parent. Needless, to say she was not planned. However, it may have been easier to stay married, and have a relationship with your husband when there are babies and then children to raise, as well as a house to maintain. The luxuries we have today allow us to forget that our conveniences save us not only time but labor. We cannot begin to imagine, let alone really think about what it was like to bear children, and keep these children alive while maintaining a home in the country for a woman. The repetitive work undertaken week by week alleviated only by the joy of having the young ones there, watching their bodies and personalities grow and mature to the adults they will become. The weekly schedule of laundry, ironing and mending, baking, the daily cleaning and tidying of the living areas and kitchen, the thorough cleaning that must be done regularly because of the man and children and the messes they create; childcare, three meals a day, hauling water and keeping the fire burning in the, generally wood or coal, stove; all these things took time out of each day. Then there was making the family garments and seasonal preserving of fruits, vegetables and meat. And the work extended to the outside as well, taking care of the garden, poultry and livestock; if the family had them, as well as the actual planting and harvesting of the food. There was no time or reason to be afraid of spiders, snakes, cats, rats or dogs. Rather they were just taken care of in whatever way was appropriate. It did not matter if it was spring, summer, fall or winter the work must be done. Elsie certainly must have had fortitude.

INVISIBLE WOMEN

Elsie Busby's occupation on the 1900, 1910 and 1920 Census was listed on as 'none', while Lawrence worked as coal miner and 'loader' working in the coal mine. Men could drink, frequent the tavern, or do nothing more than provide income or not, and yet there were very few reasons that a wife could have any control. It was not common for women to file for divorce. If they did there would have to be extenuating circumstances.

Women had no separate, legal identity. Every little thing a woman did was under the authority of the husband. He controlled all the money, including any dowry or inheritance she might have brought into the marriage. And she only had certain or limited legal rights to a share of the property when her husband died. Regardless of being responsible for the feeding, cleaning and medical care for everyone in the household as well as the cellar, pantry, and areas for preserving food and duties such as washing. Many women also kept a vegetable garden, cared for the poultry, and if they had them, milked the cows as well as making the clothing, candles and other staples, she still had no legal rights. I do not believe my great grandfather was ever abusive to his wife;

however, legal statutes and societal norms allowed for husbands to exert physical power over their wives as well.

AN ESCAPED SLAVE

Elsie's Husband

Lawrence Busby with his sons, Jonah and Lawrence Jr.
c.1910

Lawrence Busby (c.1851-1920)

Lawrence Busby, Elsie's husband, my great grandfather is said to have been an escaped slave. As a result, I do not believe this is his true name. There is a story of his trying to escape and being caught; he was returned to his owner and as punishment was subjected to having part of his foot cut off, resulting in him having to wear a funny shoe.

Through research, I have found that cutting the toes off a slave, who had tried to escape was one of many measures of cruel punishments. Laws citing acceptable punishments began in "1690 South Carolina concerning runaway slaves; these laws were revised in 1712 and would periodically come up for rewriting". According to Edward Ball; author of *Slaves in the Family* the first attempt at escape merited 'whipping', for a second attempt, branding on the right cheek with the letter, 'R', a third offense one ear and for any fourth offense castration.

The story I was told is as follows: Lawrence had two sisters, one who was punished by being hung upside down in a tree when she was pregnant, and then beaten. According to family lore, he swore he would kill the master or offender [it could have been the overseer] if it happened again. It did happen again and allegedly he took a large bolo knife, or axe and cut his head off. Whatever the case, he killed the White man and escaped; presumably by utilizing the Underground Railroad, going North and ending up in Ohio. The family story holds that he was '*quite young*', when he fled from North Carolina, presumably just before or during the Civil War.

The Underground Railroad was an interconnected system of routes and safe houses rooted in the United States and used by slaves to escape into free states and Canada. It was aided by abolitionists and others expressing sympathy to the cause of slavery. In Guernsey county, Ohio there were widespread routes of the Underground Railroad, which transported slaves to safety, earlier than the Civil War. There were known stations in "Cambridge, Senecaville, Byesville, Winterset, Westland Township and several points north of Cambridge". Most likely after Lawrence arrived in Ohio he would not and could not leave; he could never return to his family or the area he came from because; he had killed a man.

Coal Mines and Miners

It is believed some of the early segregated settlements and [Black] communities, (such as Four Mile hill, by Lore City); were likely the result of coal mines in eastern Guernsey county. Small towns and settlements held people of all nationalities; including many different European nationalities that "traveled to and worked in the coal mines." "Many of the miners at the Norris mine were children and former slaves who moved to Guernsey County at the close of the Civil War and lived in some now forgotten coal mine towns".

The Gaston Mine opened in 1850 approximately three miles east of Cambridge; it was the first of seventy-seven mines in Guernsey County The last deep shaft mine, was the Rigby Mine, which closed its operations in 1947.

The very growth of these surrounding towns in Guernsey County owe their existence to the attraction of coal mines because these small towns were established for keeping the miners near their work site. "When the coal mines went out of business, the locations and the towns were totally abandoned". Craig, Danford and King's Mine were unincorporated communities. King's Mine was a coal town in southwestern Center Township. Danford had a post office that was in operation between 1872 and 1903. A post office and convenience store were also established in 1890 in Craig and remained in operation until 1909. What the miners needed was supplied within their communities.

During that time, the men probably started the day early, maybe inspecting the weather before going to work in a hot, pitch black mine, laboring to breathe until their shift was over. The daily exhausting physical labors were common of the time, and were compounded by competitions among groups, misunderstandings because of various customs and languages; as well as living in close proximate. Frustration caused by these situations certainly could not be helpful.

Frequently, as coal was pulled from the mines, men died in on-site accidents, like my relative Simeon Dickens, who died from 'a fall of stone'. Injuries happened on-the-job as well as diseases contracted from breathing coal dust often, sooner or later, resulted in death.

Elsie Dickens and Lawrence Busby

The first mention of Elsie and Lawrence is when they married,

May 1, 1884 Cambridge Jeffersonian - Busby-Dickens-On the 24th of April 1884 by E.M. Nelson, J.P. Mr. Lawrence Busby and Mis Allie Dickens both of Danford.

Researching my great grandfather has not been an easy task. This history now has all evaporated into the cycle of time; forgotten, without anything to document the few or any memories remaining. Guernsey county undulates with hills and parts of the area are extensively wooded to this day; in this area the land is something to behold. My belief is that Lawrence found solace in this place, in one of the old coal mining towns. In this relative wilderness he could remain concealed and safe. Free but hidden, cloaked in black coal dust.

I must note that Elsie's name is spelled in so many, different ways that it is almost funny. If I had not known that my grandmother was sure of her own mother's name, I might have understood, through research, what the problem was. She is listed as Alsa, Alsie, Allie, Eliza, Elsey and Elsy in various documents. She was named for her great grandmother, Elsie or as it is written on the census, Alsy.

The March 8, 1894, issue of the Cambridge Jeffersonian notes, "Craig - We understand that Lawrence Busby will move into the James Baily property soon".

I must note that Elsie's name is spelled in so many, different ways that it is almost funny. If I had not known that my grandmother was sure of her mother's name, I might have understood, through research what the problem was. She is listed as Alsa, Alsie, Allie, Eliza, Elsey and Elsy in various records. She was named for her great grandmother, Elsie, or as it is written on the census, Alsy.

Then, the March 8, 1894 issue of the Cambridge Jeffersonian notes, "Craig - We understand that Lawrence Busby will move into the James Baily property soon"

There is no mention of his wife in this 1894 entry, even though at this time Elsie would have had four children. Without an 1890 Census there is no way to know where she resided with her husband before this time/ probably Danford, which, is an unincorporated township, where they married. On the 1900 Census they are listed in Center. Elsie and her husband have been married 17 years, Elsie has had 4 children and they are all living. The residence is rented, presumably this is the place they moved in 1894. Life seemed to be moving along smoothly for the Busby family until this post which is cited in its entirety:

July 29, 1901. The Cambridge Jeffersonian: Front Page,

"THE DEAD

GRANT TAYLOR, shot through the heart, right shoulder and hip.

MELVIN SHELDON shot through stomach and left arm.

FATALLY WOUNDED

JOSEPH REEDON, shot through abdomen

MACK SHELDON, skull fractured.

Two men dead, another perhaps fatally shot, a fourth with his head crushed in and the threatened lynching of a colored man is the result of a free-for-all fight at King's mines Sunday morning. All of the men are White except one and the negro who seems to be the cause of all the trouble was the only one to escape injury.

The cause of the trouble was the alleged intimacy of the colored man, Lawrence, with Taylor's wife, which is said to have been going on for some time and at last the indignant neighbors determined to rid the community of Taylor and his wife. White cap notices were served on them to leave the place under threats of violence, if not complied with, but the Taylors paid no attention to the warnings except Taylor armed himself and threatened to shoot anyone interfering with him or wife. [A note of clarification: 'white capping' was a violent, lawless movement among farmers that occurred specifically in the United States during the late 19th and early 20th centuries. It was originally a pattern of behavior or a system of that was not legal or regulated by the law to uphold the social standards, suitable behavior and established rights. The first 'white cap' operations were as a rule targeted at those who went against community social values. Men who did not provide proper care or abused their families, those who were idle or indolent, and women who had children out of wedlock all were presumably selected as targets of an attack. 'white capping' by legal definition is the crime of threatening a person with violence. Ordinarily, members of the minority groups are the victims or targets of 'white capping'. People are threatened in order to stop or move them away from engaging in certain behavior, business, or occupations". 'White capping' statutes were enacted as a measure to control the activities of the Ku Klux Klan.]

Sunday morning Mack Sheldon met Busby on the street near the company's store and it is said, warned him that the people would not put up with his actions much longer. This made Busby angry and he struck Sheldon in the head with a rock knocking him to the ground unconscious, the blow fracturing his skull.

Melvin Sheldon, brother of the injured man and Joseph Reedon quickly appeared, and Busby ran to his house and armed himself with a shotgun and barricaded the doors and windows. Grant Taylor soon appeared on the scene and sided with the negro. This seemed to infuriate Sheldon and Reedon and all three drew revolvers and began firing, Sheldon and Reedon shooting at Taylor. Taylor fell to the ground at the first shot and while on the ground mortally wounded, emptied his revolver at the two men and then quickly reloading shot all but one cartridge at them and fell back dead, one bullet striking him in the heart another in the right shoulder and a third in the hip. Sheldon was shot in the abdomen, the bullet coming out at side of spinal cord. He was also struck in the left arm just above the elbow. Reedon was shot in the stomach.

The two Sheldon men and Reedon were removed to their homes but so bitter was the feeling against Taylor and his wife that no one would touch his body or even cover it up to

61

protect it against the fierce rays of the sun. The body was allowed to remain on the ground just where he fell until after the arrival of Coroner Vorhies and the officers and even the Coroner had to coax the men to help him remove the body to the house.

Altogether there were twenty-three shots fired in the battle. After the three injured men had been removed to their homes the miners turned their attention toward the negro and but for the fact that he was heavily armed, securely barricaded in his house and the timely arrival of the Sheriff and officers, Busby would have undoubtedly been lynched; as it was, the officers lost no time in bringing him here and placing him in the county jail.

At about 8 o'clock Sunday morning a telephone message was received at the Mayor's office from King's mines asked that officers be sent out. Sheriff Dollison was notified and accompanied by Sheriff Gallup, Marshal Wilkin and Coroner Vorhies went to the mines at once. The excitement over the shooting was intense. Busby was secured in an upper room at his house and seemed to be glad to give himself up to the Sheriff and begged to be taken away from the mines and placed in jail at once which was done Coroner Vorhies after some trouble with the miners, got them to remove the body.

Drs. Rowles Lowry, Harrison and Mitchell were also called to the mines and the injured men were attended to.

When the officers arrived, Taylor was dead and the others while still alive, the chances to recover are against them, especially Melvin Sheldon and Reedon. Mack Sheldon, it is thought will recover. Melvin Sheldon died at three o'clock this morning. The physicians have little hopes for Reedon. Taylor is an Englishman about 25 years of age, married. He came here from Bellaire some time ago and after living in Cambridge moved to King's mines. Melvin the other dead man, is about 20 years of age and never married. Joseph Reedon is also about 20 years of age and single. Busby, the negro, had one of his thumbs broken in hitting Mack Sheldon. Sheriff Dollison does not think the miners will try to molest Busby as long as he is in jail. However, he has taken all necessary precautions against an attack."

An interesting part of this story is the realization that Grant Taylor, a White man, 'an Englishman' is the person that received the white cap notice and not my great grandfather, the negro, Lawrence Busby. I really wonder what Mack Sheldon said to Lawrence Busby to infuriate him to such a degree that he assaulted him.

This article was published throughout the country and makes me wonder how Elsie felt. My immediate thoughts went to her and the children. I wonder how she reacted when he came home and armed himself and barricaded himself in the home? Was she there? Were the children home? This was Sunday morning; she could have been in church; as usual, nothing is said about the women of any of the men involved. I wonder if Elsie knew Taylor's wife.

Did she know or believe that her husband was intimate with another woman or maybe she thought something else and may have had knowledge we at this time are not privileged to know? I wonder what kind of affect this had on their children. I cannot imagine several hundred people outside my home, wanting to kill my husband, my children terrified, whether they were there or not. I do not believe that she was accustomed to this type of aggressiveness but there is no way for me to know about their social status in this area, except for the fact that her parents and family, the Dickens, had been living here for some time without any trouble, unlike her husband.

The next piece of information was given by the Cambridge Jeffersonian, in two editions dated August 8, 1901:

"Lawrence Busby was arraigned before Mayor Baxter at 9:00 Wednesday morning for a preliminary examination on the charge of assault and battery preferred by Mack Sheldon. His wife and two or three colored friends from King's came to see him and were at the trial. During the trial Busby sat quietly listened to the testimony of Mack Sheldon and smiled once or twice. His wife sat next to him. The excitement at King's mine over the shooting has died down and the physicians attending Joe Reedon now has hope for his recovery."

"Lawrence Busby, the colored man from King's Mine who was bound over from Mayor Baxter's court to the grand jury in the sum of $200. committed to bail late Thursday afternoon. Simeon Dickens, his father in law, went to bail."

Simeon Dickens was not his father in law, rather his brother in law. I suppose he could have gone on John Dickens behalf. There is no final disposition of this criminal charge as the records are unable to be found. We do know that Elsie had a child in July the following year.

There was a property sale later in the same year according to the Guernsey County Court Land Records:

October 2, 1902 Volume 71, Pg. 88 - *Clyde W. Harbon and Margaret his wife to Lawrence Busby for $40, situated in the township of Center one acre more or less except the coal that* *underlies the aforesaid lot which was sold and deeded to the Forsythe's Coal Company.*

Is it possible that this move was a result of the trouble the previous year? With a new baby in the home it does not seem unlikely. I am sure Elsie and the children probably felt safer moving away from Danford to Center township proper, inside the city boundaries.

This article shows that Lawrence was still up to his shenanigans, I know that these arrests caused Elsie much strife. This article is copied verbatim in its entirety:

"Like Crockett's Coon

Everyone is, of course, familiar with the story of David Crockett's coon hunt. Crockett was a famous hunter of his time and the story goes on that he went out in the woods at one time to hunt for coons. Coming to a tall tree he saw a coon at the top of a tree and took aim with his gun. Just then, the fable goes on, the coon saw Crockett and said: 'Don't shoot David, I will come down.' This seems to be the attitude of some of the saloon keepers in this city since the Law and Order Society has been busy. At first, they were inclined to fight, but when they got an idea of the amount of evidence against, they and what the Society intended to do they were very meek and willing to make any terms the Society would *agree to. All the fight was taken out of them and all the desired was to settle on the best possible terms. Not one of them has offered to fight a case after they had an inkling of what was before them. All they wanted to do was to settle in the best way possible and they were all willing to agree and sign papers to stay out of the business if the fines were made as light as possible. With some of the men the Society was willing to let up but with others they were not so easy, and they were given the full penalty. All of this however leads us up to what we intended to say. One day last week Mike Slayman, white, and Lawrence Busby and Perry Dickens, colored, were all arrested by Sheriff Watson on the charge of selling, etc., contrary to the local option laws and were arraigned before Justice J. C. Carver. All three plead not guilty and demanded a jury trial. They were accommodated and their trials set for the 11, 12th and 13. However, it seems, they had a change of heart and decided that the best thing they could do would be to plead guilty and threw themselves on the mercy of the court. Busby was arraigned before Justice Carver and plead guilty. He was fined $200 and costs and sentenced to spend five days in the county jail. Next morning Dickens and Slayman were arraigned and both plead guilty. The former was given a fine of $200 and costs and two days in jail and Slayman was fined $100 and one day in jail".*

67

Not much long after the above incident Elsie, Lawrence and the family experienced a parent's worst nightmare; their child died.

5 January 1904 Guernsey County, Death Record, Book 3, Page 16, line number 5, Busby Abraham, age 1 year, 5 months, 5 days, Born -Center Twp., Cause of Death- Convulsions, Place of Residence – Center.

It seems that my great grandfather could not stay out of the judicial system as the court dates continue; this time a lawsuit. It appears that Lawrence was a finally not a defendant. I have researched through the courthouse and the genealogy department at the courthouse to find this lawsuit to no avail the records have been lost in time. I do not know what it is for.

Written in The Cambridge Jeffersonian, Thursday, June 30, 1904,

Cambridge Jeffersonian (Cambridge Ohio) 30 June 1904 "Jarod E. Baily vs Forsythe Coal Company, demurrer [pleading that objects or challenges] to second defense overruled plaintiff excepts, leave to reply by July 23. Same to E.E. Baily, William Anderson, James Valentine, Lawrence Busby. Benjamin Valentine, Andrew Anderson, Jonah Dickens and H. Dickens, Sara E Leeper, Thomas W. Bailey, ten partition suits same entries in all." This article was posted on June 5, 1905 in the Cambridge Jeffersonian, "Elsie Busby vs Lawrence Busby, divorce: grounds, habitual drunkenness".

His behavior and drinking finally got the best of her and she filed for divorce, only to find she was pregnant! My grandmother, Etta saved my great grandfather from divorce; she was born in December. And then all goes quiet. My hope is that Elsie threating with the prospect of divorce put her husband in a better state of mind and on the right track to be a better father and husband. The 1910 Census indicates the family is living in Center Township on the National Pike, Elsie, married 25 years, allegedly has no occupation, however; she did have six children and five are living.

Elsie's children were *Adeline [Addie]* 1885-1956, [her husband was Elmer Elias Beall and later following his death, Thomas Theodore Kisner [who was White]. *Lawrence Theodore*, known to me as 'Uncle Pete', 1887-1971 married Marie Capito. *Nancy May* 1890-1971 [married Theodore [Switty] Jackson, Aunt Elsie's father; John W Byrd, Andrew Walker and James/Jimmy A Buford Jr.]; *Jonah Busby* 1893-1970, [was a hermit never married, no children]. *Abraham Busby* 1902-1904 and my grandmother, *Etta Busby* 1905-1982 [who married Joseph Hankerson].

The 1920 Census shows the family living in Center Township, south of the National Road. Elsie again has no occupation. She is 50 and he is 67. A coal mine must be near because their neighbors are all miners, and are born in Slovakia, Bohemia, Montenegro, Austria, Croatia, Poland and Scotland.

The Census was taken on February 4th & 5th in February and Lawrence Busby died on February 17, 1920 from Bronchial Pneumonia with the contributary, secondary cause of Mitral Valve regulations. He is buried at the Battle Ridge Cemetery.

Elsie Busby died in Good Samaritan Hospital in Zanesville, Muskingum, Ohio December 13, 1924 from Appendicitis with the contributory, secondary cause of Peritonitis. She is buried at Northwood Cemetery.

This additional article about Lawrence Busby caught my attention -

The Friday evening edition July 23rd, 1937 in the Zanesville Signal has an article that reads: *"DO YOU Remember- When Lawrence Busby, a Cambridge man, fell heir to $36,000 in 1908? The fortune was bequeathed by an unknown."*

Could this really be true? I wonder how this money would have affected the living conditions and lifestyle of the Busby family. I am curious as to what happened to the money. Surely, this amount of money, which would be close to a million dollars today, would be more than enough to last a lifetime. The Guernsey County courthouse only lists wills by the name of the person who died; I hope one day to solve this mystery.

LIVING BETWEEN DESCRIPTIONS

My great, great grandmother

Susan McDowell (1827–1910)

Susan is first seen listed by name in the 1850 in Cambridge, Ohio Census with her mother, Delilah Kinney; she is listed as 20 years old and Mulatto. This record was made on the 28 September in Cambridge, Guernsey County, Ohio. On 16 October 1850 she married John Dickens. She had eleven (11) children including my great grandmother, Elsie Dickens. She is also listed in documents as 'Susay; and 'Susie'.

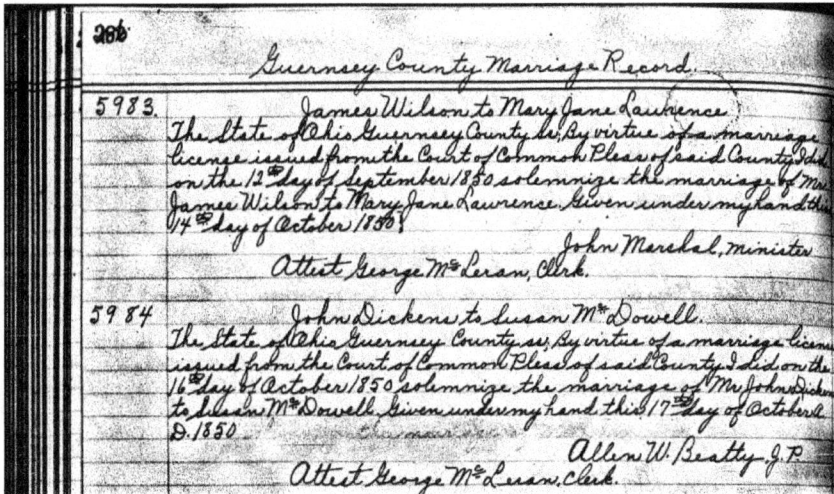

Marriage Record for John Dickens and Susan McDowell in the Guernsey County Marriage Records Book, Page 286.

Cambridge is set in the foothills of the Appalachian Mountains along I-70 and I-77. Cambridge is the county seat in Guernsey County, Ohio. It was first formed and organized in 1810 from portions of Muskingum and Belmont counties. Its boundaries were set in 1851. The countryside and woods are an example of nature at its finest.

I have included land purchases and losses, of her husband, as a way of not only tracking this family but also to give an illustration of the land they owned, bought, sold, etcetera. And I would suppose there were major life changes as a result of these property changes.

Guernsey County Courthouse, Land Records 24 November 1859 Volume 13, Pg. 549, Article of Agreement between Jonah Dickens and John Dickens by quit claim for $90 forty-seven (47) acres more or less and also part of forty-seven (47) of United States Military.

An explanation of the United States Military land: In 1796, Congress provided acreage of land to pay officers and soldiers for their services during the Revolutionary War. This area or tract is known as the

United States Military District. In Ohio the U.S. Military District and each tract contains approximately 2 1/2 million acres in Noble, Guernsey, Tuscarawas, Muskingum, Coshocton, Holmes, Licking, Knox, Franklin, Delaware, Morrow, and Marion Counties.

The divided lots entitled the owners equaled 100 acres of land; many veterans sold their warrants and a few absentee owners ever visited their land, and fewer still spent any time on it. They sold it, sight unseen. During research I found that land scrip could be bought cheaply. Its use in land transactions did not infer the holder was entitled to it by military service.

This acreage is a lot of land! However; the question I really want answered is; how did Jonah quit claim deed property to his son, John in 1859 when he died prior to 1850? Is it possible that the deed stating the land would go to his heirs was honored and a deed was procured with that legal document of the original purchase in 1837?

In 1860 Susan still lives in Cambridge and is listed as 32 and again listed as Mulatto. She lives with her husband, John and their three children. Susan has no occupation, her husband, John is a day laborer, and neither can read or write.

On the 13 July 1870 Census Susan is listed as 40 and residing in Center Township as is the rest of the family. She lives with her husband, John and is keeping house. They are all listed as White. Her husband is a farmer and owns the property he lives on. He lives next to his brother, Albert and his family. On the far right of the census is a note that reads, "Cannot attend school on account of color". I presume that these families are very 'fair' as my mother would say, and the census taker was later advised of their Mulatto or Black race. I also believe that they lived on a large tract of land and this is possibly another reason the census taker may have believed they are White.

CENTRE

Scale 1¼ Inches to the Mile

Range Nº 2   Townᴾ Nᵒ 1 & 2

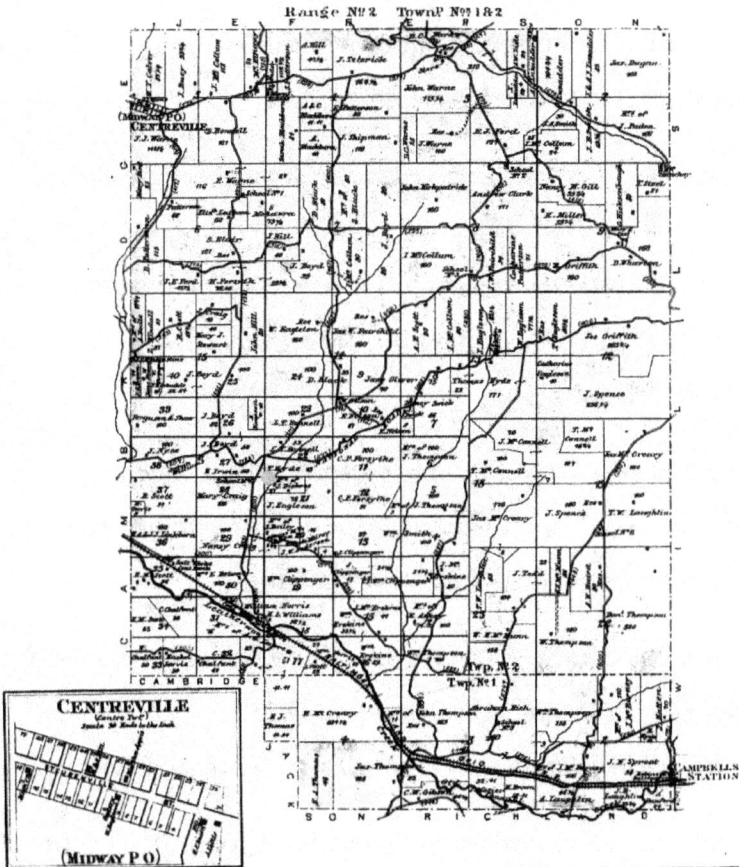

U.S., Indexed Land Ownership County Maps, 1860-1918 for J Dickons; Ohio Guernsey, 1870.

The next year John and his brother, Albert share a tract of land, as is noted in the Guernsey County Courthouse, Land Records: Guernsey County Courthouse, Land Records-Volume16, Pg. 38; 4 November 1871

John Dickens and Albert make an equal partition and division of a tract of land, being the northwest corner of lot #21 in the third quarter of the second township and second range of military lot #27 in township two of range two, one (1) acre more or less.

Several years later John buys approximately one acre as listed in the Guernsey County Courthouse, Land Records 4 September 1875, Volume 19, Pg. 548.

John Nelson and Elizabeth his wife to John Dickens for $225., situated in Center township, known as a tract of military lot #27 in township two and range two, one (1) acre more or less.

Unfortunately; three years later, both John and his brother, Albert have land sold because they are delinquent on their taxes. I am curious to know if this land lost includes the land purchased in 1859 or a more recent purchase.

3 January 1878- in the Cambridge Jeffersonian Newspaper, *Volume 46, No.34, Delinquent Land Sale, Center Twp., lists*

Dickens, Albert and Dickens, John. - Range 2, Quarter Twp. 3, Section 3, -part of lot 21, and -part of lot 7.

I have no disposition for this land; more than likely it was sold.

In 1880 Susan and her family are all listed as Mulatto. She is listed as 45 [I love this 5-year age difference from the previous census], living in Center Township with her husband, and the family all are listed as Mulatto. Her mother, Delilah Hughbanks is widowed and is residing in the household, she is listed as being 84 years old and she cannot read or write.

Once again, there is a loss of land. I do not know if this land is part of the forty-seven acres purchased by quit claim deed in 1859, but it appears to be. However, if it is that land, it was inherited from John and Albert's father, John Sr., also known as Jonah. This is very sad time for the Dickens family.

> On 4 January 1883 posted in the Cambridge Jeffersonian: "*The Lands, Lots, and parts of Lots returned delinquent by the Treasurer of Guernsey County, Ohio together with the taxes and penalty charged thereon agreeably to law, are contained and described in the following list, viz: Owner's name – John Dickens Sr, Range 2, Township 2, Quarter Twp. 3, Description, 3 pts of lot No. 21, Valuation – 157,*

Total Penalty for 1881, .86, Tax and Penalty for .55,
Total Penalty for 1882, 2.95, Total Tax - $3.81".

To my knowledge, this land was lost as a result of failure to pay delinquency.

Earlier I spoke about women being invisible despite their many responsibilities. One more thing to consider, childbearing and child mortality, even today, are two of the most serious health issues for women and their families. During this period, many people lived in the country where there were no hospitals, there may or may not have been a midwife available, yet women brought life into the world and often watched the flame of that light burn out when they had to bury their children.

In the 1900 Census in Center Township, Susan is listed as born in 1832 and is 68, [her age has changed again] she is married and is listed as Black as is the family. She and John have been married 50 years; she has had 11 children of which 6 are living. She was born in Ohio, her father in North Carolina and her mother In Ohio.

It was reported on 12 February 1903 • Four Mile Hill, Center Twp., Guernsey County, Ohio, found in the Cambridge Jeffersonian:

"It was reported on the streets Tuesday that Susie Dickens had the smallpox. She was exposed at the Quarels house but was vaccinated; Center Township Health Officer Stanley informs us that he made an investigation and finds the woman in her usual good health."

It sounds as if Officer Stanley knew my relative well.

John Dickens, Susan's son filed in Probate Court regarding his mother, 13 October 1904, Guernsey County, Ohio, an

Application of: Blind Person for Relief re: Susan Dickens, age 78.

In the 1910 Census,' Susay' is listed as Black, 85 and widowed. This date of birth is closer to her real age and may have been reported by her son, as she lives with him and is blind. John is the head of household, they reside in Center Township, number 417 on the National Pike. She has born 11 children, 4 are still living.

Susan's Children as far as I know are: *Samuel* 1849 – [before 1860], *Simeon* 1852 -1901, *He died from "Fall of Stone - Central Mine" he married Nancy Fisher; *Mary Alice* 1855-1911, *Jonah* 1858-1905, who married Francis Isaacs, *Abraham* 1860-1927, *Laura/Lottie* 1861, *Delilah* 1864 – *Elsie*

1866-1924, my great grandmother, *Eliza* 1868 - and *John* 1871-1935.

Susan's husband, John died 25 March 1910 at 91 years, of old age and Pneumonia; and Susan followed on 8 December 1910 at 83years [*take note that in the 1910 census she was 85], of Carcinoma of the Uterus. Both are buried in Battle Ridge Cemetery.

THE ENIGMATIC WOMAN

Susan McDowell Dickens Mother

My Great, Great, Great Grandmother

Delilah Jackson (c.1796-1899)

Them farther back in time you look for information, the more difficult it is to identify women outside of marriage records or an occasional newspaper article. Delilah proves this over and over for me. Absent marriage records, and records of children she is invisible. Susan McDowell's death certificate lists her parents as Delolla Jackson and James McDowell. Within these pages you will see ALL the information I know about her.

As I was finalizing this book, I did not give up on finding Delilah; however, I did say a prayer that I would have a breakthrough. I have been looking for her for many years and it seemed as though she had been erased. As I was going through old emails; I opened one from 2011 sent to me by a dear cousin, Carole, about Ned Simpson. Ned Simpson is my 5th great grandfather. As I read the entire article, I realized that I had missed some very important information:

"Cambridge Jeffersonian; March 22, 1894, page 1

LOCAL HISTORICAL SKETCHES

Miscellaneous Events from 1813 Up to the Present Time.

No. 14"

"Temperance Mitchell was one of the colored servants, and kitchen maids. She was unfortunate and had two children out of wedlock, Delitha and Asbury. Delitha took the name of her mother and married Sol Kimmy. He was the chicken killer and picker and outdoor cook confining his labors to between the kitchen and the smoke house. In these days, large quantities of pork and beef were stored for future use. Delitha was born at the old Woodrow hotel half-way between Cambridge and Washington on the Wheeling road. So, after her marriage to Kimmy [she] was a washer woman in Cambridge and the mother of Amos Kimmey of the west end, Cambridge."

I have had this information for eight years! In the meantime; before this information, I knew that Susan's father was James McDowell and she appears to be the oldest child. Delilah also had children by Edwards and Watkins. She may have been married to Thomas Watkins who was a drayman; however, I did not find marriage documents to confirm any of these other relationships. Her marriage to Solomon Kenny is verified by the following record.

The 29 July 1841 Guernsey County, Ohio; Ohio Marriages, 1800-1958.

Solomon Kenny marries Delila Watkins

I must note, that if not for this marriage citation I would have had no verification that Susan married Solomon Kenny[/Kimmy] or that he ever existed; as is the circumstance with her previous husbands. As a result of this marriage record, I later noted several mentions of him. The first entry is when Cyrus C. P. Sarchet writes about him in The History of Guernsey County:

"GENRAL WILLIAM HENRY HARRISON HERE. The first time General Harrison [soon to be the 9th U. S. President] passed through here "he was travelling east in a private coach and stopped at the Judge Metcalf tavern." The word got around that he was in town and would hold a 'levee' at the courthouse. From the tavern he was escorted and followed by a long line of citizens, many of whom were old soldiers from the war of 1812. Among these was old, Sol Kinney, colored. He had a string of buttons and a pair of bones, which he rattled and clapped being at the head of the line."

Wayne L. Snider's book Guernsey County's Black Pioneers, Patriots, and Persons speaks of many aspects of life within Guernsey County, Ohio including the following notation:

"When Sol Kimmey died, eight white men served as pallbearers. He is buried in the old graveyard" [The Old Cambridge Graveyard].

The 28 September 1850 US Census, South Cambridge, Cambridge Twp., Guernsey County does not list Sol Kenny/Kimmey. This leads me to believe he has died. There are no death records prior to 1867 in Guernsey County. Delilah Kenny, 40, is head of the household and Black; her birthplace is Ohio.

The most interesting thing about this page is that all the family is listed as Black except Susan, her daughter, who is listed as Mulatto as is Joshua R. It may be, that Joshua is Susan's son; however, additional research does not provide any answer absent a birth record.

In the 11 July 1860 Census, Cambridge, Guernsey County Delilah Kinney/Kimmey is listed, identified as Delilah Rimmey. Her age is listed as 43, [in ten years she aged three] she has no occupation; she is Mulatto. Delilah lives next door to her daughter, Susan and her husband, John Dickens and their family which are all listed as Mulatto.

I have not located an 1870 Census listing for Delilah. As far as I know Delilah's children are *Susan McDowell* 1827-1910 married John Dickens, *Amos Kinney* 1833-1925 [her stepson] a Civil War Veteran, married Martha Crable; *John Edwards* 1837-c.1880 he marries Minerva Miller, *Thomas Watkins* 1840-1930 he marries Mary A. Stryder, *Joshua R Kinney* 1849- and *Mary Kinney* 1850.

The 1880 Census shows Delilah Hughbanks, Mulatto, living with Susan Dickens and her family in Center Township, her age is 84 she is widowed. She is without occupation. I do not know where this last name is from! I wonder if it is possible that her father's name was Hughbanks or Eubanks, since we do not know, could her mother have shared that with her? Could it be in her older age she was returning to her heritage? Or did she once again marry with no records available?

I have not confirmed the below document is Delilah; however, it is the only death record I can locate and believe it probably is her, at this time. *Delilah has changed her last name so many times I would not be surprised if she used a nickname or alternate first name!*

There is no death record listed for her in Guernsey or Muskingum county. However, on 24 October 1889, Washington Daily Reporter:

"Mrs. Emily Eubanks, a colored woman, living in Dublin near Columbus, Ohio died from the effects of a dose of liniment, which she drank, mistaking it for a bottle containing cherry cordial."

Research will continue for my third great grandmother.

DELILAH'S MOTHER
My Great, Great, Great, Great Grandmother

Temperance Mitchell (c. 1800 –

From what I can tell, reiterating Wolfe, Temperance, also known as 'Tempy' was one of 'the colored servants, and kitchen maids of the 'Hutchinson house', which I presume to be an inn. As stated in Delilah's story Temperance had two children out of wedlock; 'Delitha', who is my Delilah and her brother who is named Asbury. Apparently, Asbury was born at the Hutchinson house and grew up doing all sorts of work as a 'servant'. "He learned to be a barber and had a shop in *Columbus, Ohio.* Remember, this is near where I believe his sister, Delilah, also known as Emily, died.

Wolfe writes, "Peter Jackson worked at the Hoover tavern east of Endly's. He came into Cambridge to work and here he married Tempy" Mitchell." Their married life was not altogether blissful. Pete would come home drunk, smash furniture and scatter the dishes around; then 'Tempy' would run him off. She finally left him and went to work at the Hutchison tavern where she delighted in telling guests about her 'dee vose'." It seems she fits right into my family!

Sarchet's version of their story is that "Temperance married Old Pete *Jackson* "at the old Hoover Inn kept by David Holtz, [where] the writer first saw old Pete Jackson, colored who was later a historic darkey of Cambridge. He married Tempy Mitchell, and Pete and 'Tempy' had many warm times. Pete would get drunk and try to clear the kitchen and break the dishes, and Tempy would drive Pete off. When he was asked why he did not stay with Tempy, Pete would say, 'Oh there's a coolness now but it will warm up again when the moon changes."

Sarchet continues, "Pete worked a good, many years at the Cambridge foundry, carried by Clark Robinson and B. A. Albright. Robinson and Albright dissolved partnerships and had many lawsuits. Pete was one of the witnesses. In one of the cases a question was prepared by Billy Hillyer, a pettifogging *[placing undue emphasis on petty details]* attorney engaged in the case. He stated the question to Pete and said, 'now you must answer the question, yes or no.' Pete studied a little and then said: 'I wouldn't believe that lie if I told it myself'."

SUSAN MCDOWELL'S MOTHER IN LAW

John Dicken's Mother

My Great, Great, Great, Great Grandmother

Alsy/Elsie Simpson (c.1790-c.1855)

When records were written in earlier time periods names were often misspelled as a result of the transcriber writing the name by what it sounded like to them. Elsie's name was listed as Alsy. For me writing her name this way makes it easier to know that she is the mother of John Dickens, my great, great, great, grandfather whose wife is Susan McDowell. She is the daughter of the elder Edward, also known as, Ned Simpson. Her father Ned Simpson was first seen in the Census in 1800 in Pennsylvania. While she is invisible in many ways as the other women that have come before me, I see her between the lines and in her children very clearly. She was born in Pennsylvania and her paternal story is very interesting as you will later see. Her sons, John and Albert were very close to her and looked after their mother and the land after their father died. As was discussed earlier, after her husband John died, she had no right to the land. Her eldest son, John, along with Albert took over and did what was necessary to maintain the homestead as best he could.

As far as I know, Alsy's children were: *John Dickens*, 1819–1910 husband of Susan McDowell, whom you read about previously. *Albert Dickens* 1822–1884 husband of Margaret Gilson; *Lydia* who married Richard Daniel Samuel Simpson, *Amelia* 1825–1909 who married Jonathon Gilson; *and Jonah Dickens* 1829–1865 who married Susan B. Brady, she was widowed when he died from injuries sustained during the Civil War and *Abraham Dickens* 1830–1859.

What is clear to me is that Alsy, my fourth great grandmother, had to uproot her family to move to Ohio from Pennsylvania. West Virginia was not a state until 1863. John, her husband, worked as a 'Carter', someone who took or carted people, materials, etc. from one place to another, most likely along the National Road also known as the Pike. The trip could not have been easy for Alsy and her family especially with children.

According to Wolfe, Ebenezer Zane received Government funds to cut a road from Ohio to Kentucky in 1796. *"Zane's trace*, as it was called was nothing but a bridle path through the forest. It was later widened to permit wagons, but they went at their own risk. The first pioneers used pack horses." One of the first families, Cyrus C.P. Sarchet's was "a group of early settlers from the Isle of Guernsey in the British Channel." After coming into this land they followed with a trip through and over the mountains; continuing in rainy weather and difficult travelling, as a result of following Zane's Trace, "they pitched camp in 1806 in Cambridge because the women in the party refused to move on," they would go no further.

As time went on an act for establishing a National Highway from Cumberland, Maryland to the Mississippi, was enacted in 1811 by the government. "As the first National Highway, with the first ever congressional funding for a U.S. road, the highway grew with the nation." By 1827, the Cumberland Road, also known as the Old National Pike, as well as the National Road, was 'completed" to Guernsey County, being paved with stone to Fairview and graded as far as Cambridge.

Today we have the convenience of cars, moving trucks, trains and planes. We do not ever and have to consider using horses or walking to change our residence We do not have to find a way to live on land with our families as we "chop, hew and split lumber" in order to construct a house; or making sure a water source is nearby. There had to be consideration of an appropriate amount of land to cultivate in order to seed for wheat and vegetables as well as having a safe area for horses and livestock. Finally, we must be assured that ourselves and our children are in a safe place.

The women were obligated to make sure everyone is kept warm, provide food until the planting can be done and the meat salted and stored for winter prior to their travel. The women would spin, weave and knit because nearly all, if not all the clothing was made by them. I cannot complain about my life of ease when I imagine having to bear the elements in the time it takes to construct a house.

According to an illustration in Wolfe's text; "homes of the pioneers were made of rough logs with the bark on them. He describes the construction,

"Logs were cut and brought together. Axmen stood at the four corners to notch and fit the logs as others rolled them up. After the cabin was raised it was roofed with shingles split from oak and held in place with poles or small logs. There was one large room, with a window and at one end a huge stone fireplace was built; and a chimney of sticks laid out in corn cob fashion and then daubed with clay, was raised on the outside. Wedges of wood were driven into the chinks between the logs and covered with clay. Puncheons, [short posts, especially used for supporting the roof, i.e. as in a coal mine] for a floor were made from split logs hewn smooth. Materials used for a door swung on leather or wooden hinges. Not a nail would be used in this construction."

Illustration of a wood cabin made without any nails; photo taken October 2019 by writer at Piney Woods in Mississippi.

Alsy and John must have traveled back and forth until they were settled down into an abode. During this period, it appears that they attended church. If others were living near when a settler arrived, they generally assisted him in building his cabin.

In those days the church provided the informal structure for the settlers. In this case it was the Salt Fork Baptist Church located, in Oxford Township, Guernsey County, Ohio.

"The Constitution of the church was written in 1818, under the ministry of Elder Skinner and Elder Stone. "Church met regularly, usually once a month., at the home of its members....There were no courts in that section of the county, therefore the church was the judge of rights and wrongs. Certain persons were appointed to care for the sick or elderly or to 'help out' ...the church filled the place of courts, lawyers, doctors, insurance and construction." "The original records consist of separate sheets of paper...it was assumed by the researcher the section entitled 'MEMBERSHIPS' was the list of names of members joining each year and the recurrence of names to be the children of different families. however, in 1845, there appeared to be many repetitions and notations of 'Dismissals' and 'Deaths'." The roll lists -1824 John Dickens [the elder, also known as Jonah] and John added to membership roll in 1825. John Dickins, [Sr.] as well as John Dickins and Elsey Dickins are removed from roll in 1845.

I presume the family moved because the elder John, as well as John, Alsy's husband, had died before the 1845 date and as a result Elsie and her children now reside in Center township. The 1830 Census lists John (m) [for Mulatto] aged 55-100 with 13 people in the family. Also, listed on that Census are Ned Simpson, Turner Simpson, and Benjamin Simpson; who I believe are Alsy's brothers, as well as James Lucas, Alsy's brother in law.

95

In the 14 May 1850 Census Centre, Guernsey County, Ohio records *Alsy* Dickens, 60, born in about 1790, and her birthplace is listed as Virginia. The family is listed as Mulatto. Alsy is a widow in the 1850 Census. *This is the last time I see Alsy/Elsie Simpson Dickens in a legal record.*

Throughout this book did you notice how many times the names John Dickens and Elsie are included in this family? Do you know how difficult and confusing it is to research when everyone names their children after the oldest people they remember? I think this is because of the lost history that was caused by slavery and separation and not knowing or remembering what your name really was. Repetitive first names, like anything memorized, was the only way to remember and not forget your history.

Despite the lack of writing about Alsy in texts, what I do see of her is the love of her family, illustrated by the love and care the eldest sons, John and Albert had for her. Also, I see the strength and fortitude which she had to have to move her children from one state to another during pioneer days. I also know that in 1830 she had older people in her home, presumably her mother and father in law.

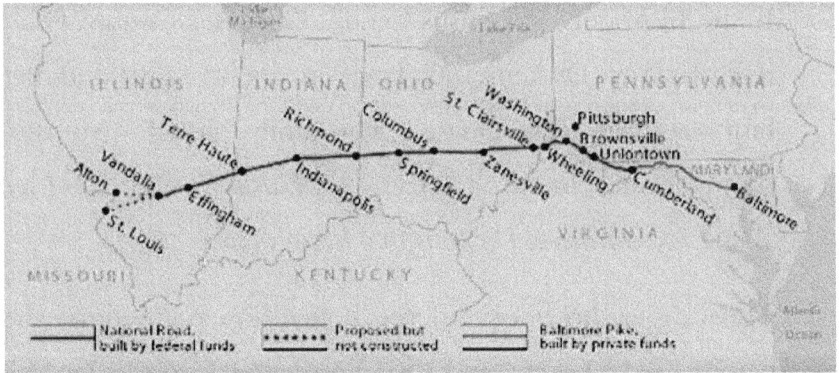

National Road constructed to Vandalia, Illinois 1811-1838.
It is approximately 620 miles. Cambridge is just east of
Zanesville. 1939 map

Alsy's sister, Edith was quite popular in Guernsey county as
was her brother, Peter. Maybe through Alsy's siblings we can
imagine a glimpse of her personality and character as well as
the living situations in Guernsey county Ohio.

Wolfe writes in his chapter, Miscellaneous Stories, *"One of
the earliest colored families to settle in Guernsey county was
that of James and Edith [nee Simpson] Lucas, who came from
Brownsville, Pennsylvania. For more than sixty years they
lived in a low-roofed cabin at the outskirts of Fairview.
Colored folks passing through on Zane's Trace and the
National Road would stop at the Lucas home for food and
lodging. Their house of entertainment was known as the
"Black Horse Tavern". Mrs. Lucas was known far and wide*

97

as *"Aunt Edie, the Fortune Teller". She possessed an extraordinary power of insight and, being shrewd, she could usually learn by clever questioning, what her patrons wanted to know, and so tell them. Her fame spread and the superstitious from all the adjoining counties would come to consult her. She practiced fortune telling for more than seventy years. Born in 1785, she died at the age of ninety and was buried in the Fletcher graveyard two miles south of Fairview."*

In 1871 Edith's Lucas' son, William was shot by Robert Wright in Fairview. Wright had trial in Cambridge before a jury composed of entirely colored men. *This was the first jury composed of entirely colored men empaneled in the state of Ohio.*

Edith's brother, Jerry was also known as Pete, or Peter Simpson. Writing of Peter Simpson, Wolfe states, *"the name will be familiar to some of Cambridge's older citizens and will call to mind the town's best-known hostlers of the 'horse and buggy days.' Fairview used to know him in the 'stage coach days".* Like his sister Peter's early home was in Brownsville, Pennsylvania. According to Wolfe, *"In boyhood Peter's love of horses drew him to the stagecoach stations where the teams were changed. He became acquainted with the drivers and some permitted him to ride with them across the mountains.*

He afterwards drove some himself and in old age never tired of telling about his perilous adventures on the old Cumberland Road." A few years after his sister and her family settled; Peter followed and became the hostler at the Bradshaw tavern. The location of the tavern stood at the east end of Fairview and was a division point for some of the stage lines. "He had fresh teams ready for the drivers when they arrived; assisted the wagoner's in caring for their horses and he directed the drivers in penning their stock for the night". Opposite the Bradshaw tavern were the coach-yard stables and sheds where Peter stored the traveler's equipment.

Peter's kind care of the horses was noticed by the guests at the tavern; "many a weary traveler was cheered by his characteristic good humor and permanent smile. Nothing pleased him more than a tavern full of guests and a wagon lot full of wagons and a barn full of horses."

When the railroad came through Guernsey county travel on the National Road declined and the tavern was sold and taken over by Morton. Morton moved to a farm in Oxford township and Peter went along to care for the horses. *"In 1873 Joseph Morton purchased what came to be known as the Morton House, for the next twenty years or more Peter Simpson was a familiar figure around the hotel."*

"When he was not sleeping, he always wore a felt or derby hat, he was touchy with requests of people asking him to remove it. When he got drunk, in his old age, he swore considerably, nobody took him seriously, as it was more of a habit than feeling." Peter never married. He loved horses and he loved children. Peter could not read or write. He didn't know his age. He was old, or older than his sister, who lived to be ninety."

Jerry Peter Simpson c. 1810-1893

My Great, Great, Great, Great Grandfather

John Dickens (c.1782-c.1845)

In the 1810 Census, John Dickens Mulatto is found in Redstone Township although the location is listed as Brownfield, Fayette County Pennsylvania. The writing along the side of the page verifies the above location. I find it interesting that some on this page are listed as Negro. John is the only Mulatto. This description leaves me to believe he had a very light complexion. The copy of this census is not clear and not well lined up. Either the entry lists none, designated by a dash, or the total number of people is 4; I am inclined to believe he was alone.

I used tax records to identify when John Dickens appeared in Fayette County as well as how long he stayed. If he was released from slavery, he would be approximately twenty-eight (28) years old in 1809.

I would like to remind you that names were written as they sounded to the person that was transcribing the information; therefore, it is not unusual to see a spelling other than one that was common or one you might expect.

These records also show that he paid taxes in Pennsylvania as well as Ohio. It is possible at some point he went back and forth moving his family slowly until his homestead was established.

These are the tax and census records that I located in Pennsylvania:

1809 Redstone Township, Fayette, County, Pennsylvania-Property Roll- Names; John Deacons, Negro-Occupation/Labor, Value $20-Horses (1) Cattle (8) [remember names were spelled by how they sounded].

1810 Redstone Township, Fayette, County, Pennsylvania-Property Roll- Names; John Dickens- Occupation/Labor, Value $8 -Horses (1) Cattle (8)

1812 Redstone Township, Fayette County, Pennsylvania-Property Roll-Name John Dickens Occupation Laborer – Horses (1) Cattle (8), value $20.

1813 Redstone Township, Fayette, County, Pennsylvania-Property Roll- Names; John Dickens- Occupation/Labor, Value $10 -Horses (1) Cattle (8)

1815 Redstone Township, Fayette, County, Pennsylvania-Property Roll- Names; John Dickens- Occupation/Mullatto man + Labor, Value $10 -Horses (1) Cattle (8)

1816 Redstone Township, Fayette, County, Pennsylvania-Property Roll- Taxables. Names; John Dickens- Occupation-Carter, Value $10 -Horses (1) Cattle (8)

The Census record for Washington, Fayette County, Pennsylvania 7 August 1820 enumeration lists for *John Dickens* a total of all persons, including White, Slaves, Colored and other at 8.

Alsy and John would have been included in this census as well as at least one of their children. I wonder if they had other children who did not survive or whether this census might have included siblings of John's or Alsy's family. This census might also have included John's father, John/Jonah and possibly his wife, who I do not know by name.

The following census and tax records were in Ohio.

1828 Civil Place Oxford Township, Guernsey, Ohio – John Dickens (Black) paid taxes on horses,[1] and cattle [2] for a value of $16.00 Total taxes $51.80

1829 Civil, Place-Oxford Township, Guernsey, Ohio - - John Dickens (Col) paid taxes on the same as above for a value of $16.00. Total taxes 4.40.

1832 Civil, Place Oxford Township, Guernsey, Ohio – John Dickens (Col) value on horses, [2] and cattle [2] a total of $16.,

Total value of property - $96. Additional taxes for Personal property - State, $33.5 County, $43.2 School, Road, $19.2 Township $9.6, - Total $105.60

Oxford Township is in Guernsey County, which is one county east of the border of West Virginia. During this time period West Virginia did not exist so travelers went from Pennsylvania directly into Ohio. Forty-seven Black and Mulatto families were reported in the Census of 1830 in Guernsey County.

1830 Census, Oxford, Guernsey, Ohio – John Dickens lists a total of all persons (Free White, Slaves, and Free Colored)-13

In the History of Guernsey County Ohio by Col. Cyprus P. B. Sarchet, Volume I, page 188; I found the following notations:

"The National road was completed and piked out as far west as Zanesville in 1830. For several years after its completion it was difficult to keep the travel on it. Heavy logs had to be laid on the sides to force the travel on the stones, so that the great throng of travelers with unshod horses avoided it as much as possible. Only the wagons and stage horses were shod. Here was a stretch of land of four miles that was preferred to the pike. The McCollum stand was not a tavern but a place where movers stayed as were most of the houses and cabins on the

on the old road. *In summer it is a much more pleasant drive
than the pike which is a little over a mile south.*"

Sarchet continues,

"*As you go up the run, then called Dudly's run, a short
distance from Jonathan Dickens' (colored) place, son of
Jonah Dickens, was where old John Chapman had his hut.
Old John Dickens and old Ned Simpson were the early
colored settlers of that region, and in the palmy days of the
Endley tavern they were hostlers and bootblacks, shining the
travelers' boots at night, making them glisten as their own
countenances, just as when a darky's face has been rubbed
with bacon rind.*"

By this time Alsy and John and their family have established
themselves and they are finally settling down enough to buy
land. I wonder if these records reflect the land where they are
residing prior to purchase?

From the Guernsey County Court Land Records,

19 April 1837 from William Beymer and Sarah his wife for
$150., to *John Dickens and his heirs* a certain tract or parcel
of land the west half of lot #21 in section 3, township 2 and
range 2 containing forty-seven acres (47) more or less.

Land Records from 29 June 1837 L/236-238 - from Thomas Watkins to John Dickens and Elsa his wife, for $75., a certain tract or parcel of land the west half of lot #21 in section #3, township 2 and range 2, containing twenty and a half acres, (23 ½) more or less.

The notation in the April 1837 estate sale is very important. It means the land John Dickens purchased did not have to go through probate rather pass from father to son(s). This is the reason I can find no documentation for the death of the elder Dickens or a property change until 1859. It could be that Alsy died on or around that time and with respect for his mother, ownership by John was then established.

On the 1840 Census, Centre, Guernsey, Ohio – John Dickens - lists the total of all persons - free White, Free Colored, and Slaves- 11.

Farming is the only occupation listed for Black men in Center Township in the 1850 Census, with a number owning property: Alsy Dickens, 60, property owner John Dickens, 25; Jonah Dickens, 21, Benj[amin] Simpson, 48, property owner, Benjamin Simpson, 21; and Peter Simpson.

As you can see looking at the family history many of the family stayed in Center Township for many years. Obviously, listing Alsy as a property owner was an error; however, this verifies to me that John, her husband had died. Although listed on the census as the head of household; her son John or Albert were likely the legal owners of this land at this time.

In 1850 on 14 May, in Centre, Guernsey County Ohio, Alsy Dickens, 60 is recorded as being born about 1790 in Virginia. The family is listed as Mulatto. Along with Alsy's children Margaret [Gilson] Dickens is listed on this census as married to Albert Dickens, their children, Lydia and Martha are also in the household. Many times, it took years for the Justice of the Peace to come along to perform marriages. In the meantime, families set up and children were born, and the ceremony would occur later if at all. There are no documents to verify the death of Alsy or her husband John.

SLAVES IN THE FAMILY

AN UNKNOWN WOMAN My Great, Great, Great, Great, Great Grandmother

An unknown woman and Edward/Ned Simpson (c.1759-)

Edward Simpson was born circa 1759 in Prince George, Maryland. His mother is known as Old Catherine born circa 1742.

To the best of my knowledge the children of Edward/Ned Simpson were *Thomas* c.1785, *Alsy/Elsie* c.1790–1859, *Turner* c.1790–1873, *Edith/Edy* c.1793–1874, *Benjamin Chandler* c.1802–1883, *John* c.1804-1884, *Jerry Peter Simpson* 1810-, and *William Edward* 1811-.

Research done in northern states, for families that are not White, follows a different manner of research; especially if their families/ancestors were free prior to the Civil War. Memories and oral history were not passed along, at least in my research, regarding slave times does not or rarely exists. Unfortunately, this leads the descendants to tell stories to justify their color and hair; many tell their children these are the result of Indian, especially Cherokee blood in the family.

This occurred because Pennsylvania and other New England states abolished slavery much earlier than the period before the Civil War. Certain records can be very useful in this instance; I have located one family member on an 1800 census, Edward/Ned Simpson, my 5th great grandfather, and I also have knowledge that Thomas Simpson was manumitted [released from slavery] in 1792.

In 1780, Pennsylvania passed a law that provided for the gradual abolition of slavery, making Pennsylvania the first state to pass an act to abolish slavery. Children *born after that date*, in Pennsylvania, to slave mothers were considered legally free, but they were bound in indentured servitude to the master of their mother *until the age of 28*.

In 1782, the abolition act was amended after the border between Pennsylvania and Virginia was settled. Those slave owners living in some parts of Westmoreland and Washington counties [and Fayette the next year] were, prior to the amended border, living in several counties in Virginia. After this amendment it was officially compulsory for slaves to be registered in Pennsylvania. For the full text see: "Act for the Gradual Abolition of Slavery, 1780," Pennsylvania Genealogical Magazine #44 (2006): pps.229-34; as well as Statutes at Large of Pennsylvania from 1682-1801 (Harrisburg: Pennsylvania 1896), 10: 67-73.

Margaret Goe was born August 19, 1727 in Prince George's County, Maryland. She was the daughter of Henry/Harry Goe and Mary Boyd Bateman. She married before 1762, to Richard Hutton. Margaret had one child: Mary Hutton who married Hezekiah Magruder. After her daughter's and son in laws death Margaret inherited their slaves. *Margaret Goe Hutton was the largest slave holder in Fayette County.* Her 12 February 1795 Will lists twenty-six slaves by name, gender, and age, sometimes with additional details.

In the 1790 census of Fayette County Washington Twp., PA, Margaret Hutton: one free White female, head of family, seven other free persons; 24 slaves. She is a widow.

In her 12 February 1795; proved 28 March 1797 WILL ABSTRACT

Margaret [Goe]Hutton, widow. "Being desirous of settling my worldly affairs at a time when it hath pleased Almighty God to bless me with sound disposing mind and memory."

This document mentions: her only brother, and his 14 children with mention of some by name, and her grandniece. The land tract she now lives on and the handling of such; she reserves ¼ acre around the remains of her daughter, and only child along with her husband, and where she wishes to be buried; as well as, *"a plot forever reserved as a burial ground for all such slaves who have been the property of my aforesaid son in law Hezekiah Magruder, deceased, as well as those who have been my own and also their offspring"*

"My slaves: Old Jeremiah, a Negro man slave, aged more than 50 years for whose own good I will add the same advice which I have repeatedly given him, viz: 'Utterly forsake that vile hussy free Chole with whom he now lives in open adultery and all his other wicked practices brought about by her advice, acceptance and secreting', Edward SIMPSON, a Mullato man slave, A CARPENTER, aged more than 36 years (has children), OLD CATHERINE, a negro woman slave aged more than 53 years (EDWARD SIMPSON is her son).....' [capitalizations are mine].*

There are three versions of Margaret Goe Hutton's will at the Fayette County courthouse: the original, a recorded copy in the will book and a rerecording of the will book. Margaret Hutton's will, Recorded copy, in Fayette County Wills 11:112-18.

Old Catherine was a slave of Margaret Goe-Hutton's father, William, therefore it appears that she was born in Prince George's, Maryland. Edward/Ned was Old Catherine's son. She was given to Margaret's daughter, Mary upon her father's death; and of course, she was inherited by Hezekiah

Magruder, her husband, in Virginia where they lived, upon his wife's death. With the death of her daughter and son in law, Margaret Goe Hutton inherited all the slaves.

What I do know is that my Elsie Simpson Dickens was very 'fair', and Edward, her father, is listed as Mulatto rather than negro, on Margaret Hutton's will. Obviously, there is more than a little cream in his coffee. But whose is it? When Margaret Hutton died it appears that her slaves were released. She had retained these slaves, her property because, it appears, they were slaves for life as a result of being born outside of Pennsylvania.

PART TWO

MY FATHER'S MOTHER AND HER MOTHERS

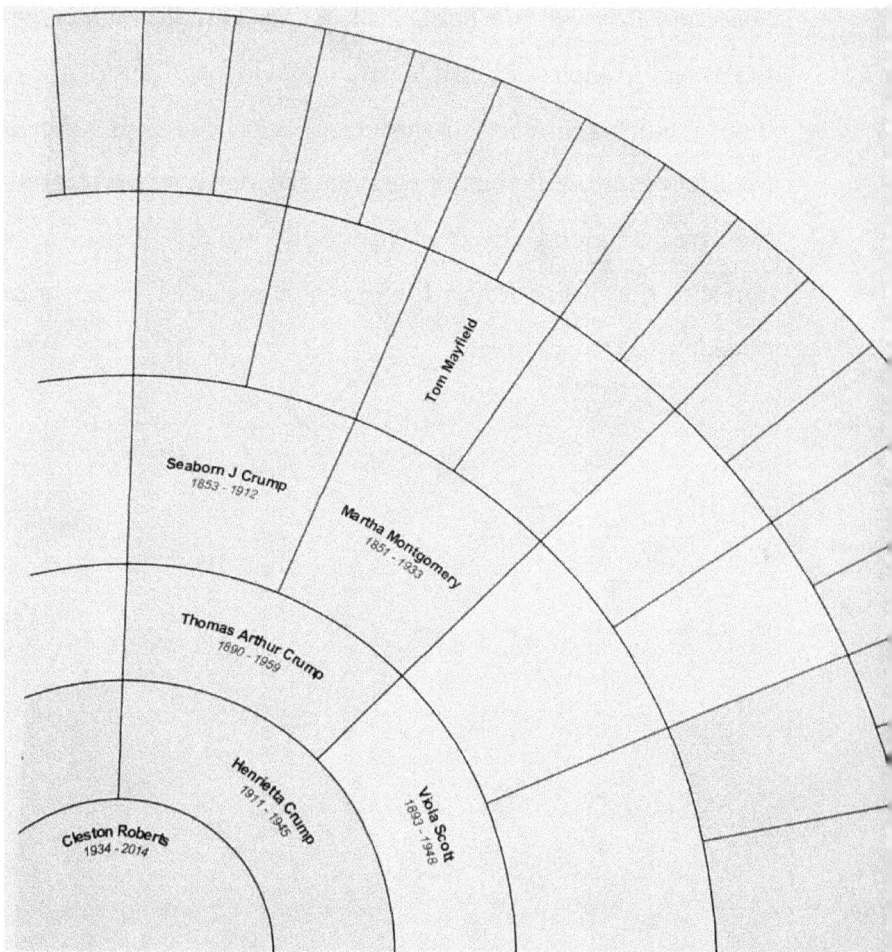

Tom Mayfield

Seaborn J Crump
1853 - 1912

Martha Montgomery
1851 - 1933

Thomas Arthur Crump
1890 - 1959

Henrietta Crump
1911 - 1945

Viola Scott
1893 - 1948

Cleston Roberts
1934 - 2014

Henrietta Crump circa 1932

Henrietta Crump Roberts with her children, Cleston, my
father and June, my aunt. circa. 1934

THE GRANDMOTHER I NEVER MET

Henrietta Crump (1911-1945)

Henrietta was born in Gainesville, Hall County Georgia. She is the oldest daughter of her parents Viola Scott and Thomas Arthur Crump. If she had lived, I would have been her third oldest granddaughter. The below picture is when she was a girl playing in the woods with her father and sister. Her parents must have moved from Georgia, when she was young. The 1920 Census shows Henrietta living in Detroit, Michigan with the family; which includes James and Henrietta Crump Wheeler, her aunt and, namesake; and her husband; along with Arthur Crump, her father, Viola, her mother and siblings, Thelma, and Thomas. Thomas Arthur Crump is her father's legal name although on many documents 'Arthur' is used.

Henrietta, her father, Thomas Arthur Crump and sister, Thelma circa 1916

In the 1930 Census Henrietta lives in Detroit on Greenlawn Street with her parents she is not employed. Two years later Henrietta marries Jehu C. Roberts, an autoworker on 20 August 1932. The following year they have my Aunt June, followed by my father, Cleston in 1934. I do not know what happened in the marriage. I do not know what was experienced; mental, physical or verbal abuse. What I do know is on 7 April 1939 Jehu, Henrietta's husband is granted a divorce on the grounds of *'Extreme Cruelty'*. Her children are 5 and 4 years old. It appears that she moved back to her parent's home because the 1940 Census shows Henrietta living on 8 Mile Road in Detroit. She has an additional sister,

Jean and both of her children in the household and she is not employed.

Unfortunately, on 4 January 1945 Henrietta [Crump]Roberts died of "Intestinal obstruction, gangrene of small bowel-Duration 9 days. Other contributary causes- Vasculitis, small bowel-2 days, December 7, 15 ft small bowels, gangrene. December 16 Bowels extruding through [illegible]. No autopsy was performed.

Her cause of death sounds like a horrible, and was an excruciating, drawn out way to die. I suspect she may have had an autoimmune disease that I have inherited from her. Daniel J. Wallace, M.D. writes in The Lupus Book, that "Mesenteric Vasculitis, Infarction and Bowel Hemorrhage is one of the most serious complications of Systemic Lupus. This condition carries up to an 80 percent mortality rate." During this time period Lupus was a death sentence for most that were diagnosed and all that were undiagnosed.

As a result of Henrietta's early death, I have few stories about her which were relayed or passed down to me through my father and other relatives. Henrietta was the oldest daughter and named after her aunt. Henrietta and her mother were closely tied together, as only a mother and oldest daughter can be, and unfortunately both died young.

117

This left my father, Cleston Roberts without a woman, no mother or grandmother to provide love and support. He constantly ran away from his father and his stepmother, who made him sleep in the basement; and his paternal grandmother, Sena, his father's mother and to his aunts on whichever side of the family he could find them, always seeking assurance and the affection that only a woman can provide.

After my grandmother's death, my aunt, June was sent to Piney Woods Boarding School, twenty-one miles southeast of Jackson, Mississippi, which she hated! The Piney Woods Country Life School was established in 1909. It encompasses 2,000 acres, and the campus includes a 300-acre instructional farm, lakes and managed timberland. Some of the first students were children and grandchildren of former slaves from the area. It must have been difficult for a northern city girl to feel comfortable in a totally foreign environment. Aunt June went from the city to farm and woodlands. Without family or friends, her mother dead, she was alone.

When June returned to Michigan, she sought love and solace from my grandmother's sister, Elaine. Aunt Elaine acted as a mother, friend and advisor especially to my aunt June and to my father. After I was born, my mother kept in touch with Aunt Elaine and her daughters. I was reintroduced to her and her daughters when I was older. I re-established close relationships with her daughters, who reminded me that they pushed my carriage when I was an infant, their live baby doll. I began to look at Aunt Elaine as a grandmother figure. She was the glue that held the family together.

While Henrietta's life on paper is scarce, I have many pictures of her, especially with her mother, and her children. I have heard that she had diabetes. I cannot confirm or deny this although it may be the reason she did not work, other than raising her children. It is clear from the many photos I have that she loved her children and at one time her husband.

Jehu holding daughter, June and Henrietta holding son, Cleston. circa 1935

Henrietta Crump Roberts and Viola Scott Crump prior to 1945

DIVORCE RUNS IN THE FAMILY

My Great Grandmother

Viola Scott (1893–1948)

As you will see, there is very limited information available for my grandmother, Henrietta, or regarding her parents. I was not close to this family until I was older. Not only does death separate a family but also divorce. My mother's, my father's mothers' divorce and death, and my great grandparents' divorce breaks the chain. Relationships are not firm as a result, families fall apart.

Viola Scott, my great grandmother's childhood story is a puzzle I have been working on for quite some time. I am hoping to one day be able to solve this through DNA. What I have heard is that Viola and her mother lived in the woods in a hut or something that would have resembled one in Mississippi or Louisiana. Her mother, allegedly, worked for a White family during the day and came home in the evening. One day she found her mother dead. She went to that family's home and they took care of her, the name of the family, I was told was Carwell or Burwell.

I presume I see Viola in the 1900 Census living with George and Millie Scott in Vicksburg Ward 4, Warren, Mississippi. Her birthdate is listed as January 1894 and she is listed as a 'Godchild' and is 6 years old. In research you frequently find the dates of birth are inaccurate.

In any case, I do find Viola in the 21 April 1910 Census. She is living with a Mattie P. Robinson in Gainesville District. Viola is listed as a servant doing housework in the home and is listed as a ward; she has not attended school, according to this record; however, she can read and write. It is stated that she and her parents were born in Georgia. It is also noted that she is deaf and dumb. Which she was not.

Enter Thomas Arthur, he lived in Gainesville as well as Viola. He was born in 1890 and listed with his parents in the 1900 Census as well as working as a Porter in 1910. I do not know how they met. However, later in that same year on 12 September 1910 in Hall County, Georgia Viola marries Arthur Crump. She is 16 years old [turning 17 on the 23rd of September. I have heard that Thomas Arthur could not stand the cruel manner that she was treated so he married her 'to get her away from that White woman'.

Arthur registered with the draft 5 June 1917, Gainesville, Hall County, Georgia. He reports that he has a wife and two children. It is clear from this notation that they now have a family; Henrietta and Thelma have been born.

The 6th & 7th of January 1920 the Census was taken in Detroit City, Michigan. Arthur and Viola, 24 and their children, are listed living with his oldest sister, Henrietta and her husband on Sherman Street. Viola says her and her parents were born in Louisiana. This may or may not be true it is the first time I see this claim noted by her. I wonder if she in fact gave this information or was it someone else.

On the April 5, 1930 Census Viola 34, and her husband and children are living on Greenlawn street in Detroit. She states she was born in Mississippi as were her parents. She is without occupation. It continues to cause me strife when I see women listed with no occupation; she had nine (9) children at this time! Her daughter, Jean, her last child, was born in 1934.

On 4 February 1938 Viola, after twenty-eight (28) years of marriage, filed for divorce in Wayne County Michigan. The divorce was granted on 15 June 1938 the cause was 'Cruelty and Non-Support' of their ten (10) children who are listed. She was granted alimony at $12.00 a week. The certificate was filed 5 August 1939 in Circuit Court, Wayne County, Michigan.

The 4 April 1940 Census Detroit, Wayne, Michigan lists Viola as the head of household, along with her children, and her daughter, Henrietta and her family. They live on 8 Mile Road. She is divorced and her age is listed as 43. She says she was born in Mississippi and lived in this same place in 1935. Now her occupation is listed as building attendant at a public school.

On another note, her ex-husband, Thomas on the 1940 census lists him as widowed. He is living on 28th street with his sister, Mary, and is working as a contracted plasterer. I imagine having one's wife divorce you might be embarrassing to tell a census worker. I have found that many wives list themselves as widowed when in fact they are divorced. This is my first instance of finding a man that claimed being a widower.

Viola died 9 October 1948 in Detroit, Michigan of "Vascular Heart Disease, (Rheumatic), Myocardial Failure, contributing factors-chronic Nephritis. Ironically, I have chronic Nephritis as a result of Systemic Lupus; a coincidence or no?

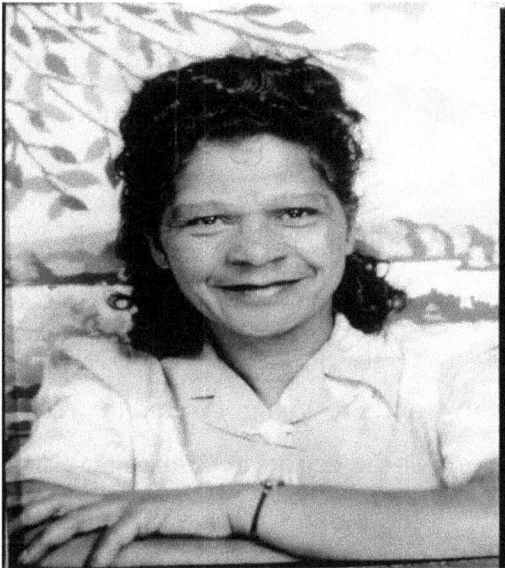

Viola Scott Crump c.1940-1948

FROM SLAVE NAME TO FAMILY NAME
My Great, Great Grandmother

Martha L. Montgomery (c.1851-1933) and her husband, Seaborn J. Crump (c.1853-1912)

The 1880 Census taken at Carnesville, Franklin, Georgia was the first I saw of Martha Montgomery Crump, my 2nd great grandmother. She is listed as 28 years old and her occupation is keeping house. Her husband, Seaborn Crump, 26, is listed as a farmer. Their children are Leander [Lee Andrew] 8, George F. 4 and Luther J. ½ a year old. I periodically run a Google search on my relatives, it just seems like the most convenient way to do research as records are added daily into repositories. One day Martha and Seaborn popped up as a match.

I was quite surprised to see in the Georgia State Archives, an abstract, in the loose papers, of their marriage license from 1873. Eventually I took a road trip to the archives with my genealogy companion, my mother. When I found the roll of film containing the record of the certificate and/or license. I asked the librarian if she could pull it for me. She informed me that the records were only those of White people; I informed her they were my second great grandparents and I wanted to see the record. They were married on Christmas Eve, 1873. When she returned, with the record it was not marked indicating race. However, the most surprising part for me was a notation along the side that said, "Terms cash in future 50 cents due by [December 31] Thursday, or certificate will not be filed". _It appears my folks got married on credit!

As I explained earlier, sometimes the Justice of the Peace or the Minister did not come around very often. Therefore, when the entry was made on the 1880 Census in Carnesville, Franklin County, Georgia of them being married since 1871 it is because that is when they established their relationship and began having children, certifying it legally later.

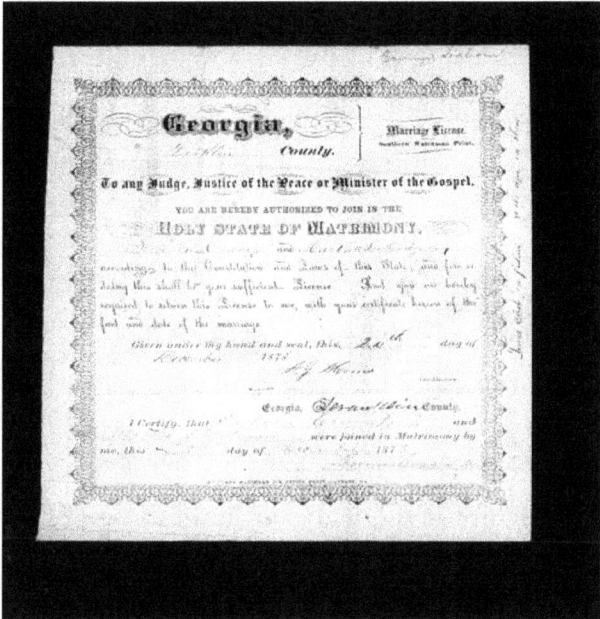

Marriage Record for Seaborn J. Crump and Margaret L. Montgomery

Twenty years later the 7 June 1900 Census was taken at Gainesville City, Hall County, Georgia, on East Washington Street. According to this record Martha is born in September 1858 and her occupation is washing and ironing. Her husband, Sebran was born in March 1857 in Georgia and he is working as a Teamster. A Teamster is defined in several ways; the first is a 'truck driver' and the second seems a precursor to a truck driver; supply trains were made up of wagons, horses and mules, teamsters were the drivers.

I would like to once again note name spellings – Seaborn, Sebran, Sebone, and Debone, as well as S.J. are all used for my second great grandfather. Crump, Cramp and Crup are common spellings and/or transcriptions. I must remember that how they heard it determined how it was written. Also, how it was transcribed often means the difference between finding a record or not. Sometimes you just must examine the entire roll. Martha and Mattie are used interchangeably.

I would also like to mention that their age never stays the same, it seems the older she should be the lower the age listed. This seems to happen with all the women in my family on both sides! My Big Aunt Mae, my grandfather's sister, once told me, "A woman who will tell her age will tell anything". I took heed; therefore, it is just not up for discussion. Although I am grateful to have lived this long, many do not.

There is another point I would like to note, Martha's daughter Henrietta would have been born between 1880 and 1900 along with another unknown child to make a total of ten (10), that unknown child must have died. Henrietta appears on no Census, that I can find, prior to 1920.

The April 20th, 1910 Census was taken in Gainesville, Ward 3, Georgia. This record shows Martha occupied as a *Laundress,* living on South Road Street. She has been married to her husband for 31 years and bore 11 children, of which 9 were living.

Seaborn Crump was born on the 10th of March 1854, according to his gravestone and died on the 3rd of May 1912, at 58 years old. He is buried at the Alta Vista Cemetery located in Gainesville, Hall County, Georgia. I had difficulty identifying when Seaborn died. I must thank my cousin, Carolyn for her diligence in locating his resting place. Later, his gravestone was photographed for Georgia, Find -A- Grave and placed online. The cause of death is unknown as death certificates were not required at that time.

Seaborn Crump Headstone 1854-1912

On the 8th of January 1920 the Census of Gainesville, Hall County, Georgia lists Mattie Crump, 59, widowed, living on Race Street. She is working as a Laundress at home, as is her daughter Mary. Her other daughter, Nellie also lives with them and is a Teacher at the Colored School.

Ten years later, on the 10th of April 1930 Census in Detroit City, Wayne County, Michigan; living on 28th street, Mattie, is widowed and employed as a Laundress. Both of her daughters live with her. Her daughter, Mary also works as a Laundress and her other daughter, Nellie is employed as a Servant for a Private Family.

On the 22 of October 1933 Martha/Mattie Crump dies in Detroit, Wayne, Michigan. Her death certificate states she died from Myocarditis. Her death record states she was born in Connersville [Carnesville], Georgia. Her mother's name is unknown, and her father's name is listed as Tom Mayfield.

Research follows paths from the present backwards with the knowledge that when you reach the 1870 census, for those that are not White, you will have difficulty as a result of the changes from slavery to freedom. I have reached a brick wall, a place where I must stop and try to find a way into slavery records; or into slave owner records in order to locate my family. The Crump, Mayfield and Montgomery families lived in close proximation to each other in Carnesville during the time Martha and Seaborn were married.

I did locate the inventory papers, for the largest slave holder in Georgia, Rhoda Crump. I came upon the will administration documents, when I visited the Georgia State Archives some time ago. To be holding these papers with my gloved hands put me in a state of awe. Looking at the burnt edges realizing how fortunate I was that these papers even existed. It was a once in a lifetime experience.

It was amazing that every cow, horse, mule and slave was listed by name. Seaborn's parent(s) may have been among these slaves. I took as many pictures, without using a flash, because it is not allowed, as possible. Some are blurry but with patience I will have them transcribed. My next genealogical road trip will have to include both Carnesville and Gainesville, Georgia. I will have to spend more time researching the Crump, Montgomery, and Mayfield slaveholders. By researching their lives, I may be able to put the history and herstory together of those that came before me. I must remember that my ancestors never could foresee anything close to the life I live, in their wildest imagination!

As I said in the introduction, I decided to divide this text into two or more books based on the incredible amount of information that I had between my four grandparents' families and their forebears. Some history will always be lost with the passage of time, swiped from our memory, the missing pieces of my identity. It is impossible to know everything. In a family, based on what you know about your people, it is easier to imagine how they lived, worked and the emotions they may have felt, or even endured when you hear their stories. The way to find history is to look to the past be it by the stories our ancestors left, or the DNA and/or memories contained in our blood. With diligence and fortitude some lost history can be found.

To Be Continued

ACKNOWLEDGEMENTS

While this book is a belated birthday gift to my mother; I would sincerely like to give my thanks to my husband, Herman, Sr. as well as my granddaughter, Shaléna, who provided the art tree design for the cover, for their patience and consideration. I did not realize the time and effort it would take to write this story. I would also like to give acknowledgement to Carole Clarke for her genealogical expertise. Thank you to my cousin, Carolyn Davis for her steadfast determination in finding and providing photographs as well as locating Seaborn Crump's gravesite. My sincerest thanks to Mary Murillo, she has been a first-rate editor and this text would not be what it is without her. Mary has been a great inspiration to me. I especially would like to give accolades to Deana Craft of the Guernsey County courthouse. Her assistance over many years has been invaluable and her steadfastness has helped me un-erase the women in my family. I would like to thank all those who have provided encouragement and proofreading, and technical support, my hero, Chris Jaeger at QuikPrint as well as Antonio Gallegos. I finally would like to thank Kathy Lynne Marshall. By proofreading her book, Finding Otho, The Search for Our Enslaved Williams Ancestors, I began to think about my own health and mortality. I realized my work would be in vain if nothing remained for my descendants. I am looking forward to writing the next text.

Those who do not look upon themselves as links connecting the past with the future do not perform their duty to the world."

Daniel Webster, 1782-1852

NOTES, RESOURCES and REFERENCES

Cover tree design by Shaléna Harris

Inside page art – Owens; Proof 106/150 **MID DAY JOURNEY, CAPE HATTERAS, HAITI.** Photograph by Robin A. Roberts Harris 2019. Art work is in my personal collection.

INTRODUCTION

Note -regarding 'outside children' the man could be taken to court for the illegitimacy-by force of the mother's sworn testimony, the man was usually adjudged the putative father and was compelled to enter into a bond with sureties, to support the child at a set amount; currently DNA is used verify paternity. However, in some states if the woman is married her husband assumes parentage and responsibility for the child.

Costello Sue; Author. This poem was shared in its entirety on Facebook page: 'Hope's Seed', Accessed 5 July 2019.

Information was located and photocopied at the Guernsey County Courthouse located at 801 Wheeling Avenue, Cambridge, Ohio 43725

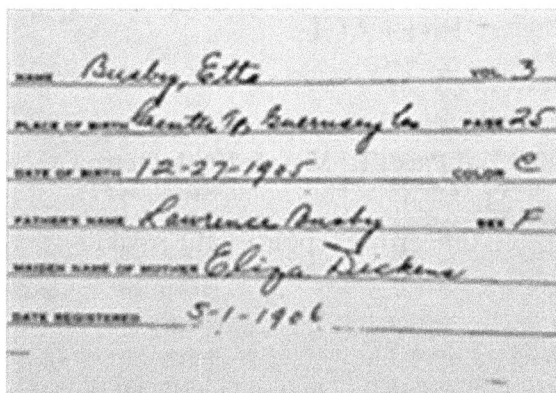

*Note mother's name

The Guernsey County Genealogical Society is located at 125 N 7th St, Cambridge, OH 43725

The Family History Library on Temple Square is the largest genealogical library in the world. It is located at 35 North West Temple, Salt Lake City, Utah 84150.

African Ancestry, 5 September 2008 Identified Haplotype HV, a non -African lineage. www.africanancestry.com

LET'S TALK ABOUT DEFINITIONS

Pew Research Center, Social and Demographic Trends; What Census Calls Us: A Historical Timeline.
https://www.pewsocialtrends.org/interactives/multiracial-timeline.

PREFACE

Officer Down Memorial Page; 12 March 1989, Detroit Police Department, Michigan. https://www.odmp.org/officer/6780-police-officer-vikki-elaine-hubbard

Note- For more information regarding Carl Jung review- Analytical Psychology: Its Theory and Practice (Routledge Classics) Revised Edition, 2014, by C. G. Jung, (Author)

Signe, Dean. Scientists have observed epigenetic memories being passed down for 14 generations- Science Alert. 27 April 2018, article accessed July 2019. https://www.sciencealert.com/scientists-observe-epigenetic-memories-passed-down-for-14-generations-most-animal

Carey, Benedict- Can We Really Inherit Trauma? New York Times, Headlines suggest that the epigenetic marks of trauma can be passed from one generation to the next. But the evidence, at least in humans, is circumstantial at best. 10 December 2018. Accessed at: https://www.nytimes.com/2018/12/10/health/mind-epigenetics-genes.html

Khazan, Olga – Inherited Trauma Shapes Your Health: A new study on Civil War Prisoners adds to the evidence suggesting that our parents'-and even grandparents'-

experiences might affect our DNA. 16 October 2018 The Atlantic; Article. Accessed July 2019. https://www.theatlantic.com/health/archive/2018/10/trauma-inherited-generations/573055/

PART ONE

MY MOTHER AND HER MOTHERS

Note-My first book was Alice in Wonderland by Lewis Carroll given to me by my Aunt Sharon for my birthday.

An Escaped Slave –

Lawrence Busby-My Great Grandfather

Van Horne-Lane, Janice; 2011, History Press. Safe houses and the Underground Railroad in East Central Ohio.

Still, William, Finseth, Ian, Ed. 2017, The Underground Railroad: Authentic Narratives and First-Hand Accounts and Still, William; 1868 The Underground Railroad, Volume 1, Philadelphia, PA

Snider, Wayne L., 1979, Guernsey County's Black Pioneers, Patriots, and Persons, Ohio Historical Society.

Major, Noah P. The Pioneers of Morgan County, Memoirs of Noah J. Major, Indiana Historical Society Publications, Vol. V, No. 5.

Forte, Jim, United States and Worldwide Postal History-Guernsey County.
https://www.postalhistory.com/postoffices.asp?task=display&state=OH&county=Guernsey & jimforte@postalhistory.com

Guernsey County Historical Society.
https://guernseycountyhistory.com/2016/05/06/rocks-that-burn-to-the-gilded-age-how-coal-mines-built-guernsey-county

Ohio, Guernsey County; 1884 This marriage is noted on page 396 n the marriage records. The license application is dated April 23, 1884 and the certificate of marriage is dated the 24th day of April 1884 joined by E.M. Nelson.

 U.S. Legal; accessed online:
https://definitions.uslegal.com/w/whitecapping

Also see Meyers, David & Meyers-Walker, Elise; Lynching and Mob Violence in Ohio, 1772-1938.

State of Ohio, Bureau of Vital Statistics, Probate Court, Certificate of Death, File #11929, Volume#3197, Guernsey County filed 17 February 1920 for Lawrence Busby, Date of Birth 20 March 1852, Age 68, Occupation Miner; Birthplace North Carolina, Name of Father and Mother Unknown, Birthplace of Father and Mother Unknown

State of Ohio, Department of Health, Division of Vital Statistics, Certificate of Death, File #68359, Volume #4618 filed 19 December 1924 for Mrs. Elsie Busby. Date of birth not listed, Note "about 58", Occupation Housekeeper, Birthplace Ohio, Name of Father: John Dickens, Birthplace of Father Ohio. Information for mother is not known. * Elsie was in fact 58 years old, having been born in 1866.

Living Between Descriptions

Susan McDowell My 2nd great grandmother

Ohio, County Marriages, 1774-1993, Guernsey County Marriage Records - 1842 - 1861 Pg. 286, record #5984, 17 October 1850 for John Dickens to Susan McDowell. Accessed Online: www.ancestry.com

State of Ohio, Bureau of Vital Statistics, Certificate of Death, Guernsey, County, Center, File # 14157, Filed 26 March 1910 for John Dickens. Birthplace Ohio, Occupation Farmer, Father's Name: John Dickens, Mother's Name: Elsie Simpson.

State of Ohio, Bureau of Vital Statistics, Certificate of Death, Guernsey County, Center, File #66315, Filed 11 December 1910. Birthplace Ohio, Occupation Housekeeper, Father's Name: James McDowell, Mother's Name: Delolla Jackson.

The Enigmatic Woman

Delilah - My 3rd Great Grandmother

Wolfe, William G., Stories of Guernsey County Ohio; History of an Average Ohio County, 1943

Year: 1840; Census Place: Londonderry, Guernsey, Ohio; Page: 357; Family History Library Film: 0020165. Entry for Thomas Watkins

Ohio, County Marriages, 1774-1993. Marriage Date 26 Jul 1841. Marriage Place, Guernsey, Ohio, USA Number000317295. www.ancestry.com

Sarchet, Cyrus Parkinson Beatty, History of Guernsey County, Ohio, Volume 1. B.F. Bowen & Company, 1911, Indianapolis, Indiana accessed on line, 2015 - https://archive.org/stream/historyofguernse01sarc/historyofg uernse01sarc_djvu.txt

Susan's Mother in Law

Alsy/Elsie Simpson Dickens My 4th Great Grandmother

For more information on the National Road see - Hulbert, Archer B. (1920). Johnson, Allen; Jeffreys, Charles W.; Lomer, Gerhard R. (eds.). The Paths of Inland Commerce: a chronicle of trail, road, and waterway. (online digital auto-scanned reproduction) (Textbook). and The Chronicle of America Series (Textbook ed.). New Haven, Toronto, London: Yale University Press.   Accessed online: https://babel.hathitrust.org/cgi/pt?id=mdp.39015062381333&view=1up&seq=13

The National Road - Back in Time - General Highway History - Highway History - Federal Highway Administration. www.fhwa.dot.gov. Retrieved 2019-02-25.

Williams, T. F., The Household Guide and Instructor, with Biographies, History of Guernsey County, Ohio with Illustrations. Windmill Publications, Incorporated, 1882

Conner, Robert Mrs., The Salt Fork Baptist Church, Guernsey County, Oxford Township, Ohio was located on Baptist Road, Twp. Rd. 693.

1820 U S Census; Census Place: Washington, Fayette, Pennsylvania; Page: 116; NARA Roll: M33_103; Image: 12, 6 - Free Colored Persons - Males - Under 14, (3) Free Colored Persons - Males - 26 thru 44, (1) Free Colored Persons - Females - Under 14, (2) Free Colored Persons - Females - 14 thru 25, (1) Free Colored Persons - Females - 26 thru 44, (1) Number of Persons - Engaged in Agriculture-(3) Total Free Colored Persons-(8) Total All Persons - White, Slaves, Colored, Other-(8). Accessed online -www.ancestry.com

1830 Residence place: Oxford, Guernsey, Ohio, United States, for John Dickens. Free Colored Persons - Males - Under 10 (4) Free Colored Persons - Males - 10 thru 23 (2) Free Colored Persons - Males - 24 thru 35 (1) Free Colored Persons - Males - 55 thru 99 (2) Free Colored Persons - Females - Under 10 (2) Free Colored Persons - Females - 36 thru 54 (1) Free Colored Persons - Females - 55 thru 99 (1) Total Free Colored Persons 13 - All Persons (Free White, Slaves, Free Colored)-13

1840 Census, Centre, Guernsey, Ohio – John Dickens. Free Colored Persons - Males - Under 10 (2) Free Colored Persons - Males - 10 thru 23 (2) Free Colored Persons - Males - 24 thru 35 (1) Free Colored Persons - Males - 36 thru 54 (1) Free Colored Persons - Females - Under 10 (1) Free Colored Persons - Females - 10 thru 23 (2) Free Colored Persons - Females - 36 thru 54 (1) Free Colored Persons - Females - 55 thru 99 (1) Persons Employed in Agriculture (2) Total Free Colored Persons (11) Total All Persons - Free White, Free Colored, Slaves- 11. Assessed online www.ancestry.com.

Year: 1850; Census Place: Centre, Guernsey, Ohio; Roll: M432_684; Page: 173; Image: 101.

PART TWO-

MY FATHER'S MOTHER AND HER MOTHERS

The Grandmother I Never Met-

Henrietta Crump

Michigan, Marriage Records, 1867-1952; license #411397 on 15 August, Marriage on 20 August 1932. 2015 www.ancestry.com

Michigan Department of Community Health, Division for Vital Records and Health Statistics; Lansing, Michigan; Michigan. Divorce records; Michigan, Divorce Records, 1897-1952. #77399, docket #284,981. 2014; www.ancesty.com

Michigan Department of Community Health, Division for Vital Records and Health Statistics; Lansing, Michigan; File Number: 331488. Michigan, Death Records, 1867-1952 [database on-line]. Provo, UT, USA: Ancestry.com 2015.

Wallace, Daniel J., M.D. The Lupus Book: A guide for patients and their families. New York, Oxford; Oxford University Press, 1995; pp. 133-34.

Piney Woods Boarding School https://pineywoods.org/

Viola Scott-My Great Grandmother

Georgia, Marriage Records from Select Counties, 1828-1978, Viola Scott, Marriage Date-21 Sep 1910, Hall County, Georgia; Spouse [Thomas]Arthur Crump. www.ancestry.com

U.S. Lists of Men Ordered to Report to Local Board for Military Duty, 1917–1918 www.ancestry.com, Arthur Crump, Entrainment Date19 Sep 1917, Entrainment Camp Chamblee, Georgia Local Board Bleckley, Georgia, USA 1917.

U.S. World War II Draft Registration Cards, 1942. www.ancestry.com

Michigan Department of Community Health, Division for Vital Records and Health Statistics; Lansing, Michigan; Michigan. Divorce records. Michigan, Divorce Records,1897-1952. State Office#78583, Docket #2760719

granted 15 June 1939; Circuit Court, Wayne County,
Michigan.

Michigan Department of Community Health, Division for
Vital Records and Health Statistics; Lansing, Michigan.
Michigan, Death Records, 1867-1950, for Viola Crump,
Death 9 October 1948; File Number000884, Local File
#12161. *Death Certificate notes - State of Birth –
Louisiana, the informant was her daughter, Violet*.

From Slave Name to Family Name

Martha L. Montgomery My 2nd Great Grandmother

Georgia, Franklin County, 1873 24 December. Marriage
Record for Seborn J. Crump and Margaret L. Montgomery.
Georgia State Archives, Franklin County Marriages, loose
records. Acquired in 2008.

Michigan Department of Community Health, Division for
Vital Records and Health Statistics; Lansing, Michigan.
Michigan,

Death Records, 1867-1950 for Martha Crump died 22
October 1933. File Number 175573, Local File Number
10666. The informant was her daughter, Mary.

---

www.ingramcontent.com/pod-product-compliance
Lightning Source LLC
Chambersburg PA
CBHW070631030426
42337CB00020B/3980